PERIOD SHIP
MODELMAKING

PERIOD SHIP MODELMAKING

An Illustrated Masterclass

The Building of the American Privateer

Prince de Neufchatel

PHILIP REED

NAVAL INSTITUTE PRESS
ANNAPOLIS, MARYLAND

∽ *Author's note* ∽

In my previous book there was a final section of photographs of the finished model along with a separate colour section, either to view separately or refer to as reference whilst building a model. In this volume the photographs of the finished model have been dispersed throughout the text, as far as possible to illustrate areas of the model being covered at that point. They are easily distinguished from the text photographs by the linear border around them. A selection of further models, good examples of small craft, are displayed at the end of the book.

Copyright © Philip Reed 2007

First published in Great Britain 2007 by
Seaforth Publishing
An imprint of Pen & Sword Books Ltd
47 Church Street
Barnsley
S Yorkshire S70 2AS

Published and distributed in the
United States of America and Canada by the
Naval Institute Press,
291 Wood Road, Annapolis,
Maryland 21402-5034

Library of Congress Control Number: 2007930352

ISBN-13: 9781591146759

This edition authorized for sale only in the United States of America, its territories and
possessions, and Canada

Printed & Bound in China through Printworks Int. Ltd.

Contents

Building the Privateer
Prince de Neufchatel

❦ *Introduction* ❦

Several years ago I built a model of the 74-gun ship *Majestic,* and at the time of building took numerous photographs, captioning each, and finally presenting them in book form as *Modelling Sailing Men-of-War.* The aim was to take the reader step-by-step through the process of building the model and I hoped that the book might be of general interest to period ship modelers while offering detailed advice to those wanting to build a model of a similar subject.

In the Introduction I explained that many of the methods outlined in the book could be equally well adapted to my more usual scale of 1/192 (16ft to the inch), and certainly could be modified for building a smaller and simpler vessel, which might appeal to the less experienced modeller. However, I must admit that, if I were now where I was thirty years ago, I might find the wealth of complex detail on a 74-gun ship somewhat daunting and the process of extracting and utilising the relevant information really quite difficult.

This all came to mind recently when I was commissioned to build two 1/192 models of the *Prince de Neufchatel,* the American schooner-rigged privateer. One was to be full-hulled and coppered with bare spars and displayed on a cradle, and the other a waterline model under full sail, set off against a carved sea. It occurred to me that I could produce a second book that could stand alone as a guide to building a small and rather simpler flush-decked vessel, or could be used in conjunction with the first book as a more general manual for those interested in this subject of miniature modelling. The advent of digital photography made the task all the easier as I was able to take photographs and prepare captions simultaneously, as each stage of the job was completed.

In a number of photographs a ruler has been included which is not just to give an idea of scale but to help the reader understand that the finished model looks quite different from the impression given by many of the close-up photographs, which might suggest that some of the detailing is a little crude. The distinguished ship modeller Donald McNarry believed that miniature models should never be portrayed at a larger size than the models themselves, and I tend to agree with him. Doing so rarely shows off to advantage any virtues the model may possess but magnifies the tiniest of blemishes and faults. It is, however, something that I have resorted to repeatedly in these pages in order to show better the methods used to build them.

A small flush-decked vessel, fore-and-aft rigged, such as a schooner or cutter, presents the miniature model builder with one of the simpler prototypes, both in terms of hull construction and rigging. There is no need to hollow out and detail below decks except, that is, immediately below any open companion way or hatch, and that is optional. The actual hull shape itself is certainly a lot less complex than that of many larger vessels with their tumblehome, wales, rows of gun ports and often extensive decoration at the bows and sterns. These simpler craft are an ideal choice for anyone new to the discipline.

I have built several other small models to the same scale of 1/192. Three of them are American vessels, *Lynx, America* and *Washington* – though the former was captured and taken into the Royal Navy and renamed *Musquidobit* – and two were British, the cutter *Surly* and the brig *Grasshopper.* I have included these vessels in the book, showing them as finished models, to give the reader a better idea of the variety of ship types to be tackled. The core of the book depicts the building of the two models of the *Prince de Neufchatel* herself, and between them they demonstrate just about all of the techniques used to build these other models.

*   *   *

The American privateer schooner *Prince de Neufchatel* was built by the Brown brothers of New York in 1813. She was one of a new class of large, fast and seaworthy schooners that first made their appearance during the War of 1812. She had a short but notoriously successful career that earned her a permanent place in her nation's history.

On her completion she was sent to Cherbourg, France, under the command of her captain, J Ordronaux. In March 1814 she put to sea and captured nine prizes in the English Channel, and for the rest of that summer she created havoc amongst enemy shipping. Seventeen times during this period she was pursued by British men-of-war but always managed to evade capture due to her speed and sailing qualities. In September she returned to Boston for a short refit.

Just one week into October found the *Neufchatel* at sea again, already in company with a new English prize, when she was spotted, becalmed, by the British Frigate *Endymion.* The *Endymion* was unable to get alongside before darkness fell, so she sent in five of her boats carrying between 111 and 120 men to cut out the schooner. Although the *Neufchatel*'s small crew numbered only forty they managed to fight off their attackers after a very bloody twenty minutes, with, however, great loss of life on both sides. The *Neufchatel* then managed to make her escape along with her prize and return to Boston.

On 21 December the *Neufchatel* was at sea once again, but just five days later she was sighted by the British frigates *Newcastle, Leander* and *Acasta.* After a long day's chase she was finally captured, but only because she lost some of her spars, damaged under too great a press of sail. After her capture she was sent back to England, and would have been taken into the Royal Navy were it not for an accident in dry dock when she broke her back on the sill of the gates. She was broken up in 1815. Displayed as a model some two hundred years later, her slender lines and the elegant rake of her masts conjure up for another generation those wild chases across the open seas.

∽ *The Masterclass* ∽

Before making a start on the model it is, of course, absolutely necessary to have a set of plans to work from. In my previous book I worked from a set of Admiralty draughts and demonstrated a method of drawing up rigging plans from these. With many eighteenth– and nineteenth-century ships this will be the only course open to you. However, many of the more famous ships will now have commercially available plans produced for them, though, it must be said, of varying quality and reliability. Fortunately for us there is an excellent set of plans available for *Neufchatel*, giving lines, hull profile and deck plan, hull details and fittings and sail and rigging plans. Full details for obtaining them can be found in the Bibliography at the end of the book.

I chose to use jellutong for the hull. There are other timbers that would serve as well, but I have got used to using this; it is very stable, close grained and carves cleanly and easily.

⌒ The Hull ⌒

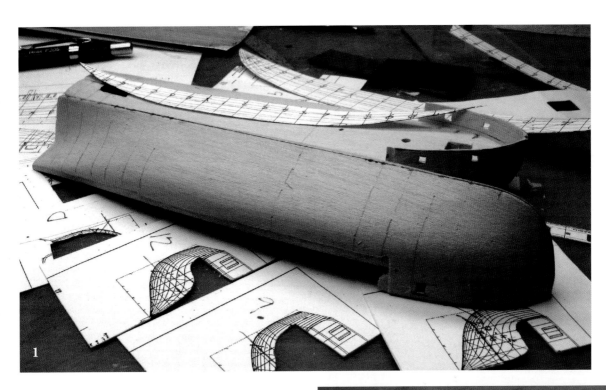

1.

After first sawing and then planing the blocks of jellutong to the correct plan and profile the hull was carved and then sanded to shape. All the templates were cut from copies of the lines plans mounted with double-sided tape on 10 thou plastic card. This stage in the work can be clearly seen in this first photograph.

2.

Because of the complex curves of the bow the forward section of the bulwarks was carved integral with the hull. This was then hollowed out with gouges and chisels. The bulwarks were finally finished with various grinders in the Minicraft tool and the deck levelled and camber introduced with a small plane, a chisel and, finally, a sandpaper block.

Gauging the exact height of the deck at the side was facilitated by drilling through from the outside at the level of the deck and flooding a little dilute water colour paint into the holes. As soon as these started to

show during the carving process it was obvious that the correct level had been reached. The blue stain can be seen clearly in the photograph. Note also the 'well' cut below the forward companionway. The sides of these wells should be lined with black paper and the bottoms with a piece of spare decking. Also at this time, holes were drilled for the masts in the decks and holes drilled in the base of the hulls for the threaded rods to be used for mounting the models.

3.

This photograph shows the forward end of the rebate for the bulwark, which was left over-thick for the time being to allow the rebate to continue up the side, so making it much easier to line up the plywood strips accurately when fitting them to the hull.

4.

Before fitting the bulwarks the decks had to be prepared. Sufficient decking material for both vessels was made up in the following way. First, some holly shavings were glued to some good-quality paper. When this was dry the paper side was treated with a coat of Seccotine and the shaving side with a good coat of clear shellac. Now the individual planks were cut from the mounted shaving and were laid up on some thin card. The glue used was Seccotine with the addition of a little raw umber watercolour to suggest the caulking. Paper templates were then prepared (one can be seen on the upper hull), these being used to mark out the decks. The rectangle in the centre of the template is there to allow the midship station line to be seen, this can then be used as a reference point for the mast holes and openings for the companionways. When the decks were cut to size they were glued in place with Evo-Stik contact adhesive.

5.

The decks are in place and some simple ply jigs have been fitted to the deck with a few spots of superglue. The glue is only applied along the centreline, where any marks that it may leave will be covered by one of the deck fittings.

6.

The ply bulwarks were glued in place, working from fore to aft, making sure that they lined up with the angle of the jigs. When the glue has set the jigs can be carefully broken free.

7.

The join between the ply and jellutong bulwarks then had to be reinforced as this is an obvious weak spot. The cutter in the chuck of the drill was used to cut grooves spanning the join, and small strips of ply were then inserted into the slots. These were then flooded with a very thin superglue, bonding and strengthening the whole structure. The forward section of bulwarks was then finally thinned, using burrs and sandpaper blocks, so removing the rebate originally used to locate the ply bulwark. This was now marked out for height and position of gun ports etc. and carefully trimmed to size. The ports were then opened up, but left slightly small at this stage.

8.

The stern was next cut from the ply, glued in place and then given the same joint-stengthening treatment as the forward end of the bulwarks.

9.

As well as the gun ports, the oar ports needed to be opened up. They were first of all drilled and then squared using this little file held in a pin vice.

10.

The next job I tackled was the fitting of the waterway. On the ship it would have been fitted against the frames and would have butted against the edges of the deck and bulwark planking. On the model I fitted the lowest bulwark plank first and then added a small triangular plank to simulate the visible section of the waterway; there is visually no difference. I manufactured the strips of triangular material in the following way. The edge of a strip of veneer was planed to a 45-degree angle …

11.

… before trimming it off on the Preac saw.

12.

13.

This photograph shows the lowest plank, or spirketting, that reaches the base of the gun ports, and the 'false' waterway.

A tracing of the stem was made from the plans and used with some carbon paper to transfer the outline to some correctly thicknessed boxwood. Then a slot was cut in the stems with a razor saw. This was then further opened up with various diamond burrs and the stems glued in place. The keel was glued directly to the hull before dowelling along its length. The final dowel has yet to be broken off.

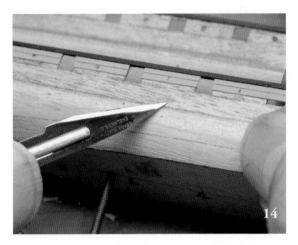

14.

A start was then made on the hull planking. The top strake was cut from some pre-painted and mounted shaving. The next three strakes (two shown here) were cut from unmounted and prepainted wood shaving as these were noticeably thinner. After fitting the two planks shown they were trimmed around the gun ports and pierced by way of the oar ports. The screwed rod in the base of this model is clearly visible here. It will be used to mount the model on a temporary work base and finally to secure it in the carved sea.

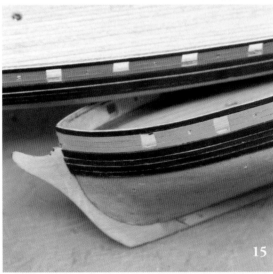

15.

The third yellow ochre plank in place along with the thickstuff above the wales and the wales themselves.

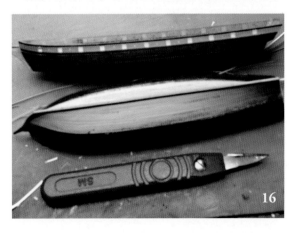

16.

The remainder of the hull was then planked. As the hull was to be copper plated there was no need to be too pernickety about the run of the planking below the waterline. I have seen it advocated that the hull planking need only extend to just below the waterline and then be faired into the timber hull. This seems to be a rather unsatisfactory solution, particularly if the true lines of the hull are to be preserved.

17.

The sternposts were then fitted. If you look carefully you will note that this has not been done strictly according to full-size practice, as the keel does not run the full length of the ship but ends forward of sternpost, but this will be invisible and of no consequence once the hull has been coppered. The counter has been planked and the rail beneath the stern ports glued in place. On the full-hull model in the foreground I have started fitting the framing around the counter. The section on the quarters was made from strips of holly, but that beneath was built up from lengths of copper wire. This is an easy way of dealing with the complex curves involved. After gluing the wire in place the area between was filled with Roket Powder. This useful filler comes in the form of a free-flowing powder, in appearance rather like very fine sugar, and is specifically for use with superglue. I find it works best with the thinner grades of superglue. The granules are sprinkled in the area to be filled and then flooded with superglue. On large areas I use it directly from the bottle, but for something like the present application I prefer to use my usual tool: a piece of wire in a pin vice. The advantage of this type of filler

is not only its strength but the instant results. Once set it can be filed or sanded to an extremely fine finish.

18.

The counter timbers have been filled, sanded and painted. As can be seen, using the wire has given a clean flowing curve around the stern. The rudder is only temporarily in place and is held with a wire pin fitted in line with the lower hinge.

19.

With the exterior planking finished, a start can be made on the coppering. The first job is to mark in the waterline, or more accurately draw a line ½in above the waterline. To do this the hull needs to be set up at the correct angle. I have placed strips of timber of the requisite thickness beneath the bulwarks fore-and-aft and am here marking in the waterline using a hard pencil. Before I came across this useful little tool I simply fixed the pencil on top of a block of wood of the required height. Minor adjustments can be made when sharpening the lead of the pencil, which should be a sharp chisel point.

20.

I used some painted tissue paper for the copper plating on these two models. Having in the past experimented with various methods, including the use of fine copper shim, I have come to the conclusion that there really is, visually, very little to choose between them. This photograph shows a sheet of prepared tissue, taped to a cutting board and being cut into strips ⁵⁄₆₄in wide, the depth of each sheet of copper.

21.

The steel ruler in the foreground has been fixed to the cutting board, parallel to the cuts, using double-sided tape. Now more cuts are made at right angles to the original ones at ¼in intervals, using the transparent set square that can just be seen beneath the knife. This process is a little trickier than it might seem, as, after the first cut has been made, the strips of tissue are only anchored at one end, so care is needed not to misalign them either when moving the set square or making the cuts. I found that a strip of masking tape applied to the underside of the square helped to keep the tissue in place while making the cuts.

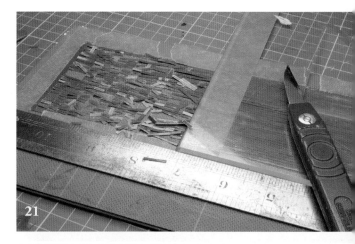

22.

The bench set out all ready for the coppering to begin. All that is needed is a sharp knife, a finely pointed pair of tweezers, dividers, sable brush, and some Seccotine.

23.

The first strake of plates have been laid and trimmed with a sharp knife, the waste being gently soaked off. The second band has just been started.

24.

As each strake of plating extends fore and aft it will, as can be seen here, curve upwards and cross the waterline. Before starting the next one it should be carefully trimmed. Nepean Longridge in *The Anatomy of Nelson's Ships* recommends that the waterline be raised slightly at bow and stern to avoid the optical illusion of it appearing to sag at either end, and I have done that here.

25.

Six strakes have been laid working downwards from the waterline and one strake has been laid alongside the keel. The remaining five strakes have been started and now it is just a matter of working steadily fore and aft.

26.

Three complete strakes are laid working upwards from the keel. These have been completed on the starboard side. From now on it will be necessary to trim some of the plates as certain strakes gradually diminish and disappear. At the stern there are also a number of stealers required

27.

The fore end of the hull with the plating completed. The keel has been drilled in line with the holes already drilled for the threaded stainless steel rods, and these have been fitted. The side of the keel has been plated and I am now in the process of working my way up the stem.

28.

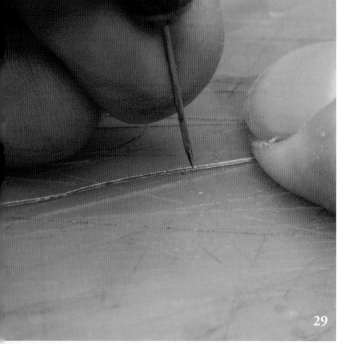

29.

28.

Keel, stem and sternpost have been coppered; plates are also laid along the underside of the keel, along the edges of the stem- and sternposts and up the trailing edge of the rudder. The hinges have also been fitted.

29.

These were made from the same copper-painted tissue as the plates. A thin strip was cut and the rivets simulated by pressing into the back of the strip with a sharpened needle in a pin vice.

30.

The next job that can be done is to cut an opening for the bowsprit. I first drilled a small hole and then opened it up to the correct diameter with this diamond burr.

31.

Now to complete the internal planking of the bulwarks. The first plank above the spirketting has been glued in place and I am trimming any unwanted areas by way of the gun and oar ports. The scalpel blade being used has been sharpened to a needlepoint to enable me to trim the latter neatly. I find I am always reshaping and sharpening many of the tools I use. It is a good habit to get into because it is just not possible to have tools and blades that are just perfect for every sort of specialist work. A good sharpening system helps immeasurably. I have recently invested in a powered tool sharpening system that has both a water-cooled grind wheel and a leather surfaced polishing wheel. It puts a razor-sharp edge on all the cutting tools I use.

32.

32.

After working my way up the bulwarks, trimming as I went, I moved on to the stern, which can be seen here planked but still with some trimming and neatening required.

ᗌ *Working Bases for the Hulls* ᗌ

33

33.

These are the two working bases I have made up for the models. The one at the back needs no description but the other, for the full-hull model, needs a little explanation. Any jig for supporting a model during construction needs to keep the model firmly and accurately in an upright position and do so without damaging the hull. Once the basic three-sided jig was assembled, holes were drilled in the base to accept the threaded rods, and two little blocks of jellutong were roughly carved to fit the contours of the hull. The inner surfaces of these blocks were then liberally coated with some model filler and a couple of strips of felt laid over them; these were further covered with some thin polythene, in case any of the filler bled through. With the hull in place, upright on the jig, the blocks were gently pressed in from either side, checking repeatedly that the model remained upright. As an aid to this I placed a 6in ruler across the bulwarks amidships and checked the height either side at the edge of the jig. When I was satisfied that all was as it should be, a few spots of superglue were applied along the edge of the jellutong supports to fix them in place. When the filler had set the model was lifted free and the polythene discarded. The little model could now be removed and replaced in its cradle whenever required without risk of damage to the delicate copper plating.

34.

With all the planking and copper plating completed, it was time for a clean-up. All the ports, both gun and oar, are given a final trim and file, checking each gun port for both height and width with a little plastic card jig. Then the whole model was given several wipe-overs with a damp cloth. For obvious reasons this needs to be sensitively done with immediate 'dry-offs' between 'washes'. This will remove all traces of Seccotine from the planking and copper plating. At this stage any of the paintwork that needs it is given a touch-up using several coats of very dilute paint so as not to obscure the delineation of the planking. Careful painting is also required around the various ports. When thoroughly dry the copper plating was given a coat of medium-oak-stained varnish to mellow and enrich the copper effect; this was followed by an overall coat of slightly diluted satin matt polyurethane varnish for protection. Later I decided to weather the copper a little with some dilute washes of Windsor and Newton's cobalt green oil colour.

35.

I frequently recall the modeller Harold Underhill's enthusiasm for plank-on-frame construction. He maintained that once you had a keel, stem and sternpost assembly you had a model of sorts, and I do agree that it is satisfying to see a model ship grow in this way. With solid hull models such as these we do not have that satisfaction, but there are compensations. There are certain stages in the building process when transformations take place, and I always feel that this is one of them. Instead of seeing ship-shaped blocks of wood and ply, two miniature hulls begin to take on the character and graceful lines of the *Neufchatel*.

⟶ The Main Rail, Channels and Pin Rail ⟵

36

36.

I decided to make the rail from boxwood, so thicknessed a plank in my Preac thicknesser, a most useful recent acquisition. Before owning it I would have used a sheet of suitable veneer. Here the outer edge of the rail is being marked on the underside of the timber.

37

37.

Once marked, the outside of the rails were cut and carefully sanded to the line; then the width of the rails was marked in with this tool. It is simplicity itself. Two scraps of wood are held in a small clamp. One of them has a rounded end and the other a small hole drilled in it, in which a short section of 0.3mm clutch pencil lead has been glued. Then the rail is carefully cut from the sheet, leaving a little to spare.

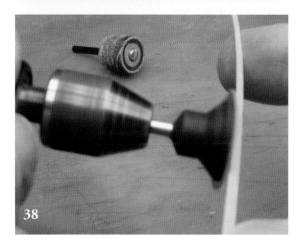

38

38.

The inside edge can then be finished with a disc sander along the side of the ship and with the drum sander, in the background (in perfect focus, unlike the rest of the picture; I am still adapting to digital technology) around the bow section.

39.

The rails are finished, but before fitting them there is one more job to be done; fitting the channels, such as they are, and the pin rails. This proved to be a very simple procedure on this vessel as they are both situated at the same level and fit immediately beneath the rail. This photo shows a groove being cut to accept the piece of boxwood that will form both channel and rail. Note the well-honed and sharpened blade.

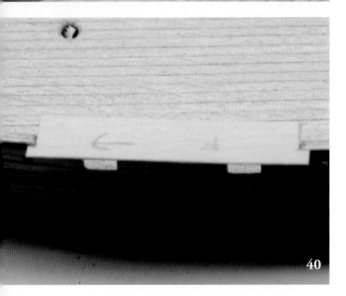

40.

The strip of boxwood cut roughly to size and glued in place. Once this had been done for all the channels on both models the rails were fitted. I used superglue for this and worked my way gradually from bow to stern, applying the glue little by little using a piece of fine wire in a pin vice as applicator.

41.

The rail glued in place. Both channel and pin rail have been trimmed and sanded to their finished dimensions, and the pin rail has been marked out in pencil ready for drilling for the belaying pins.

∽ *The Bow and Figurehead* ∽

42.

Now to move on to the head. Not a major or difficult job on a little ship like this.

The first details to be fitted are the upper and lower cheeks. These were trimmed from a sheet of card and glued in place with superglue. I started this process at the point where the hull planking meets the stem. The exact position was ascertained by measuring down from the rail, and then little by little I worked fore and aft, checking angle and curve, applying the glue, as usual, with a thin wire.

43.

Neufchatel, according to Howard Chapelle, was fitted with a coronal figurehead. But as this was indistinguishable on the original plans I have resorted to my own interpretation. I built the crown from a circlet of paper with two rings of fine wire around the outside, top and bottom. This was then filled with some modelling putty to form the velvet lining before forming the rest of the crown from more paper strips. A tiny glass bead was added to the top and a little wire shield fitted beneath it. This was then filled with a little of the putty. As you can see from the photograph it is barely ⅟₁₆in across

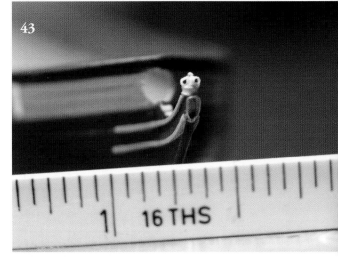

44.

The head rails and timbers, like the cheeks, were cut from card. I used quite a soft absorbent card for these, and then, when they were completed, treated them liberally with thin superglue. This creates a very strong structure that can easily be filed and sanded to a smooth finish. Artist's gesso was used to develop the figurehead further and to add a little decorative scroll beneath it. This was applied with the tip of a 0000 sable brush and built up in several layers.

45.

Strips of yellow painted tissue were next cut and applied to the rails, cheeks and head timbers. A boxwood hawse timber was shaped and fitted just above the upper cheek and the hawsehole carefully drilled through the hull so as to emerge on the inside of the bulwarks just above the waterway. Just below the upper cheek a slot has been filed ready to accept the gammoning to the bowsprit.

❧ *Deck Fittings* ❧

46.

Now to move on to the deck fittings. I am making a start with the companionways. *Neufchatel* has one forward and another incorporated in the half deck-house aft. At this stage they are simple shell constructions formed from home-produced three-ply of yellow cedar shavings.

47.

To ensure a tight fit with the deck the heavier moulding that runs round the base of the deckhouse is being glued in place *in situ*. It is here being held firmly against both deck and deckhouse with a pair of tweezers while the glue sets. The end of the moulding on the far side can just be seen. Both will be trimmed flush with the house before fitting those at the ends. The end timbers will need to be slightly curved to accommodate the camber of the deck.

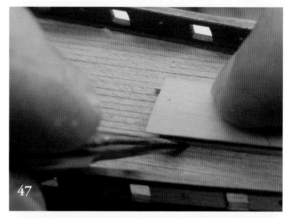

48.

The companionway forward is treated in a similar fashion, only this time, instead of sitting directly on the deck, it fits inside the opening cut to receive it.

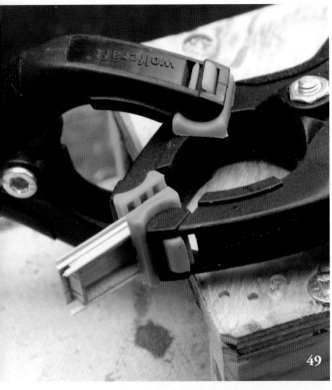

49.

While fitting the remainder of the framing it is most helpful if some means of holding these tiny fittings can be fabricated so as to allow freedom for both hands to do the work. These little clamps have many such uses, though much can be accomplished with clothes pegs, elastic bands and a little ingenuity.

50.

The panelling on the sides of the deckhouse is fitted and the positions of the skylights and companionways have been marked in and are being opened up.

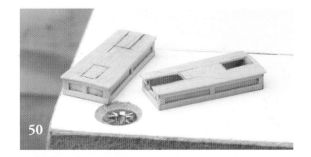

51.

The sides and ends of the skylight have been built up and the skylight glazed with clear plastic. In the foreground the two forward companionways are almost ready for their tops and doors.

52.

The sliding tops to the companionways have been fitted, along with the framing to the skylight. All this work was carried out using boxwood.

53.

The bitts are fairly straightforward to construct, as should be clearly seen in this photograph. Note the dowels carved as part of the uprights; these locate directly into the holes drilled in the deck. Again all this work was carried out using boxwood.

54.

The *Neufchatel* was fitted with small winches mounted on the fore and main bits. Here one of the wooden drums is being turned using a scrap of sandpaper.

55.

After each one is finished it is parted off with a sharp knife blade.

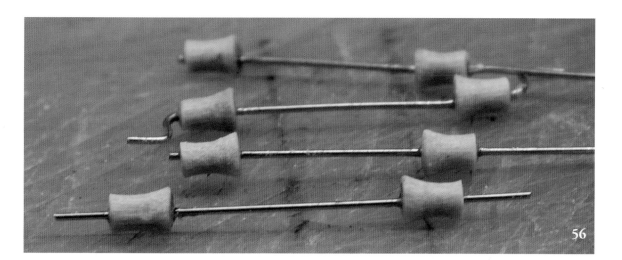

56

56.

The finished drums mounted on their wire spindles. The handles would have been removable, so only the one pair has handles made from the wire, as I do not at this stage intend showing the other three in use.

57.

Three of the completed and stained bitts with the winches glued in place. The metal plates that support the winches were made from strips of black paper.

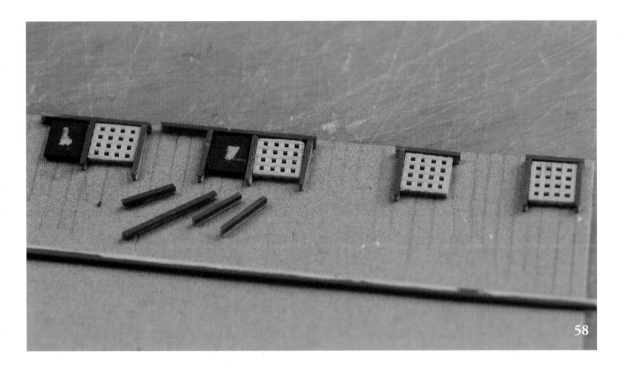

58.

Only two small gratings are required for each ship, one for the scuttle right aft and one over the galley stove. I used some left-over grating material from a previous model. This was originally constructed in exactly the same way as shown in *Modelling Sailing Men-of-War*, in which I gave detailed pictorial coverage, but I will explain here the method used in brief. The Preac saw was used to prepare the gratings and for 1/192 scale I used a 12 thou saw blade. A sheet of thin boxwood about 2in square was partially run across the saw table and then secured in this position with double-sided tape. This forms a new top to the table that fits snugly against either side of the nearest end of the blade. It is now possible to cut very narrow strips of timber to a fine tolerance and excellent finish. A guide made from 12 thou square boxwood is next glued to the new boxwood table parallel to the saw blade and exactly 12 thou away from it. The saw was then set to a depth of 12 thou and a sheet of boxwood about 2in by 5in and ½in thick was run across the saw with the shortest end against the guide, so cutting a groove in the underside 12 thou from the end of the timber. The next cut was made by running the wood again across the saw but this time with the first groove running snugly

over the guide. This process is repeated, cutting successive grooves 12 thou apart along the length of the timber. The saw blade is now raised and 12 thou strips cut lengthways from the grooved stock. These will form the cross-members of the gratings. With the saw still set to cut 12 thou strips some boxwood is run down into 12 by12 thou square lengths.

Now the grating is made up by fixing the notched lengths of wood to a board with narrow strips of double-sided tape, notches uppermost. They are attached to the tape at the ends only, and laid out parallel to one another. At either end short spacers of the 12 thou square timber are fitted tightly between them. Now lengths of the square stock are glued at right angles to these in the grooves. First, every tenth notch is treated in this way, fitting temporary spacers alongside them. When the glue is dry these spacers can be removed and the remaining lengths of timber glued in place.

The photograph shows the gratings cut to size and being fitted with their coamings. All the constituent parts are glued down to the paper backing, each being trimmed accurately to size before the next is fitted.

59.

59.

A similar technique was used for the hatches, but these were covered with boards, not gratings. I made these up the same depth as the coamings, as can be clearly seen in this photograph.

60.

When building small-scale models one of the eternal challenges is how to avoid damaging delicate or vulnerable details already completed. The catheads for *Neufchatel* are an example. On the vessel herself they would have been fashioned from carefully selected compass timber with the grain following the bend. To cut them from sheet timber would have made them very vulnerable to accidental breakage, so I glued together two sheets of 1mm modelmakers' ply and made mine from that.

60.

61.

Holes were drilled either end of the sheaves, a slot fashioned and the space between the holes rounded off using this home-made drill to suggest the sheaves.

62.

The catheads ready for a final sand before painting; note that they have been fitted with cleats for the anchor ring stoppers. In the foreground are the various timber heads that will be fitted to the rails.

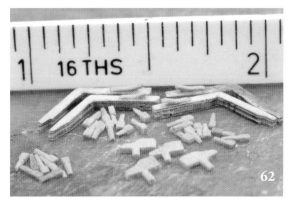

63.

A fair number of cleats are going to be needed; the larger ones were made from a strip of boxwood by the method shown here. They were then mounted on wire pins for inserting into drilled holes in the bulwarks.

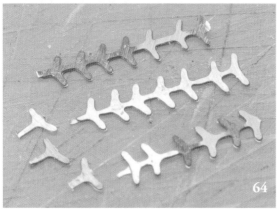

64.

For the smaller cleats I used some brass etched ones that I had made up some years ago. Before I had made these I used to make these little fittings from copper wire either by bending the wire around the circumference of the cleat with the two ends forming the pin for fitting in the bulwark, or by soldering together a small T of copper wire and then filing it to shape.

65.

For the two models at least four hundred ringbolts will be required. Some of these are for the gun carriages, some for the bulwarks and others for the deck. I have found no short cut for producing these, so they have to be made up individually. I do this initially by winding a loop around a drill shank, as shown here, then cutting away the surplus wire with a sharp knife, and finally straightening the shank with tweezers.

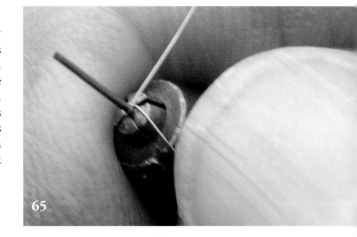

66.

Yet another repetitive job is the production of all the coils of rope required, some of which will be for the decks and others for the pin rails. Some wire is first wound round a drill shank of suitable diameter. Then several coils are cut from the resultant winding and flattened with a steel rule for use on the deck, or shaped over a pin driven into the edge of a block of wood ready for fitting to a belaying pin.

67.

The ringbolts have been mounted in strips of plasticine pressed on to battens of wood, and the rope coils also mounted on battens but by means of narrow bands of double-sided tape. Each coil should only be attached to the tape at its very edge, otherwise they will prove extremely difficult to remove without damaging them.

I now airbrush all these little fittings. It is easily the quickest and most efficient method of painting them. The only other viable alternative is to paint the rigging wire before winding the coils. I would advise against trying to brush-paint coils of rope after they have been made, as the paint will fill between the individual rope strands and spoil the whole effect.

⬱ *Guns, Anchors and Port Lids* ⬱

68.

This photograph shows a length of boxwood dowel, used for making the gun barrels, in the chuck of the lathe, with the remainder of the previous barrel turned still in evidence. The card jig determines the length of the barrel plus about ⅙in. The taper is already set and the barrel is turned in one slow cut. If the barrels are always set to this exact length they will all be turned to the same size and taper.

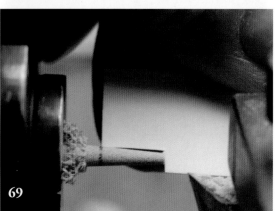

69.

The turned barrel is cleaned up with some fine sandpaper, and then a second card jig is used to determine the length of the barrel. It has been marked in and will now be parted off using a fine razor saw.

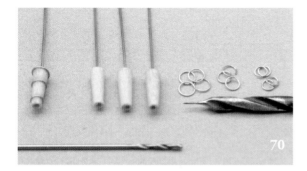

70.

The barrels are then drilled at either end with the home-ground drill and then the muzzle opened up with a small twist drill. The lengths of wire that are glued in the far end of the barrels will form a useful handle for the time being but will eventually be cut down to form the basis for the cascabel, built up finally with a little glue. The reinforcing rings are made from copper wire wound round various-sized twist drills and are glued in place with a touch of superglue. The barrels shown here are for the carronades, and for these another hole will be drilled just forward of the middle ring and a second wire inserted at right angles to the barrel; these will eventually be used to fix the carronade in place by passing them through the carriage and locating in a pre-drilled hole in the deck. The cannon barrels will be drilled and fitted with wire trunnions and will eventually be fixed to the deck, after first gluing in place, by drilling down through the vent and inserting a wire pin at this point down into the deck.

71.

The sides of the cannon carriages were made by the following method. A strip was cut from the end of a length of box producing a strip with the grain running across it. It was then shaped as shown in the picture by repeatedly running across the Preac saw, finally finishing off the curve underneath with a small file. Then sides can be sliced off, again on the Preac saw. Only four will be required but the strip can be put aside for future models. The sides are now mounted on the axles; these are allowed to protrude slightly either side and the trucks then glued directly to them. These can be turned from box, or at this scale punched from card. Short lengths of fine dowel or wire are used for the ends of the axles and they can either be glued directly in position or, as I prefer to do, drill a hole through the truck into the axle before fitting, so making a stronger fixing.

72.

The basic construction for the carronade beds. When dry the ends are rounded off with a disc sander.

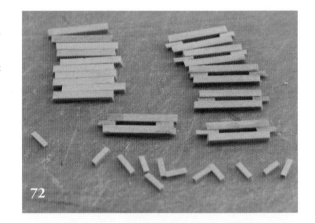

73.

The carriages have been fitted to the top of the beds and here they have been turned over and are now being fitted with the trucks. These are being cut from a boxwood dowel by rolling the dowel while pressing down with the knife. This just about completes the work on the guns apart from painting and the fitting of the required ringbolts.

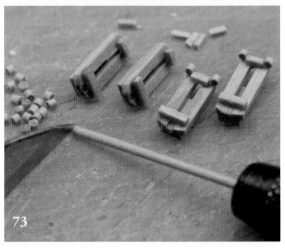

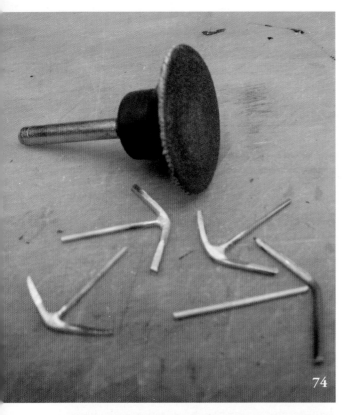

74.

I made the shanks and arms for the anchors from brass rod; these were silver soldered together and then shaped with the disc sander and small files. Anyone who has not ventured into silver soldering would be well advised to give it a try. The materials required are readily available from any good supplier of jewellery-making materials.

75.

The palms (from paper) have been fitted and stocks of boxwood constructed. When these are glued in place it only remains to make and fit the rings, paint the anchors and stain the stocks. Several coats of wood glue can be used to build up the puddening on the anchor ring.

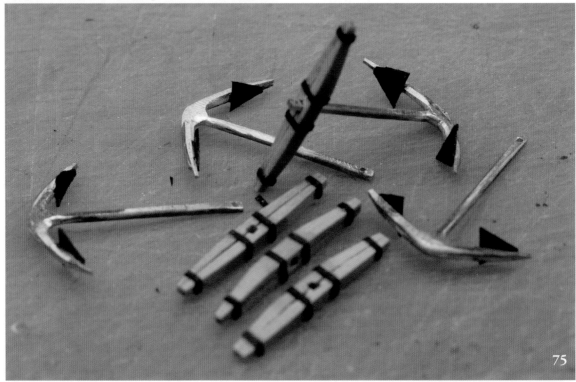

76.

76.

I chose to make the port lids from a strip of thin boxwood. This was then grooved to delineate the planking, using the cutter shown in the picture. It was made from a strip of junior hacksaw blade; a hook is shaped at the end, the point of which is then sharpened to a V. In use it is drawn gently along the edge of a steel rule several times before gently cleaning up the groove with some fine wire wool. The individual port lids are then cut off on the Preac saw. Alternatively thin card could be used, planked as the hull, and the lids cut from the strip using a sharp knife. Incidentally, the notches on the underside of the blade are used to produce mouldings from strips of boxwood; they were cut using a fine dental diamond burr.

77.

77.

The lids have been painted and are here being detailed. They have been drilled for wire hinges and ringbolts, the wire hinges will not be visible on the finished model. The hinge straps were made from pre-painted paper. One of the ringbolts is being fitted; it must now have another ring formed on the underside by winding once around the drill shank before being trimmed off.

78.

78.

Now two small holes are drilled at an angle for the wire hinges to locate in. The port lids are vulnerable fittings and so are set on one side for the time being.

79.

80.

Sweeps will need to be made to be stored on deck. They were made in the following way. A piece of boxwood a little wider than the sweeps are long, and as thick as the width of the blades, is prepared. This is now run repeatedly over the saw blade either side of the wood, leaving the thickness of slightly more than the diameter of the shaft.

The sides are now sanded smooth and the finished shape of the blades formed with the disc sander. Individual sweeps can now be sliced off, the little blocks at the ends removed and then the sweep is finished by turning on the lathe, one end at a time. The blade is then finished by hand. A finished sweep can be seen in the foreground.

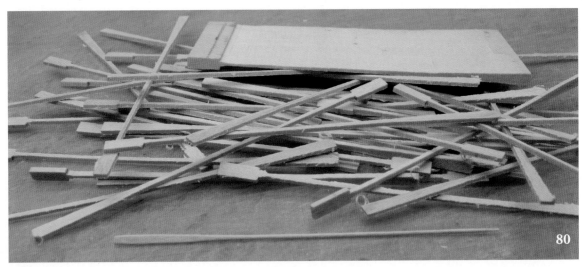

81.

Boarding pikes are also easily overlooked. They were made from fine brass wire. Each was put in a pin vice and the point sharpened by rotating it against a drum sander.

82.

Three fire buckets are required for each model. They are turned from boxwood and then hollowed with a fine diamond burr, finally being parted off very carefully with a sharp knife. The handles were fashioned from wire.

\mathcal{O}\!\mathcal{O} *Ringbolts and Ladders* \mathcal{O}\!\mathcal{O}

83

84

83.

Another lengthy job involves fitting the ringbolts for the guns. It is very important to be careful only to drill partway through the bulwark. Some modellers drill these holes before planking the outside of the hull, which is a wonderful idea if you can remember to do it.

Another feature to note here are the cleats above and just to the right of the gun ports; these are for the lanyards for raising the port lids, and they should be fitted at this stage.

84.

The ladder fitted for the stern companionway. It has been painted buff as a foundation for 'wood stain' that has yet to be applied.

85.

Boats can be built at any stage of the project. First, a wooden hull is carved from some fine-grained hardwood, using, as with the ship itself, templates for plan, profile and section. This is carved 'over deep' and with a reasonable wedge of wood left above the sheer line. Screws are then inserted in the top of the hull to form handles.

Next, a cardboard tray is made to contain the filler used for the female mould; the inner drawer from a matchbox is ideal for many of the smaller boats. The wooden male mould is now rubbed over with candle wax, the tray filled with car body filler and the male mould pressed into it till the filler is just above the sheer line. A little gentle pressure should be kept on the tops of the screws until the filler starts to go off to make sure that the wooden hull does not tend to float upwards. When set, the hull is worked free from the

filler and then sanded down all round so that when replaced in the female mould it leaves a gap of about 10-15 thou. The moulds are then ready for use.

86.

The casting of hulls in ABS plastic sheet is really quite simple, though you may find that some practice is required, and that several castings for each hull are needed before you are satisfied with the result. In practice, a sheet of plastic is placed over the waxed mould and this is held under an electric grill until the plastic softens and sags. This is not always as simple as it sounds as the plastic sheet will initially try to roll itself into a cylinder or convolute in some other way, anything other than lie flat the way you want it to. I have taken to holding it flat with a strip of wire mesh, as shown in this picture, at least in the initial stages of softening.

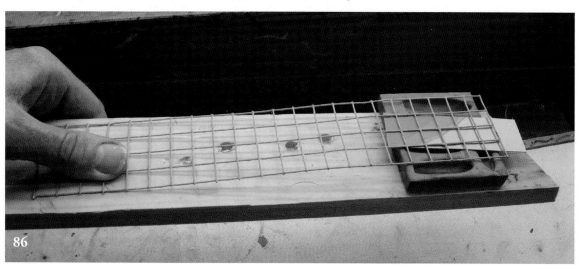

87.

88.

When the plastic has softened sufficiently the mould is withdrawn from under the grill and the male mould pressed firmly in place and held there for a few seconds while the plastic hardens.

I have so far not made any mention of the largest of *Neufchatel's* boats. The plans show an outline on her deck for what appears to be a 28ft cutter, which would be a logical choice. I had no available mould, but had one for a slightly shorter boat so decided to make use of that. In this photograph can be seen the slightly lengthened hull and the new female mould prepared for it. Although this may seem a simpler solution to the whole process it is only usable when the subject has no concave curves.

89.

The mould in use. The plastic has been softened and the hull former pressed into place.

90.

The hull form seen from below before extracting the casting from the mould.

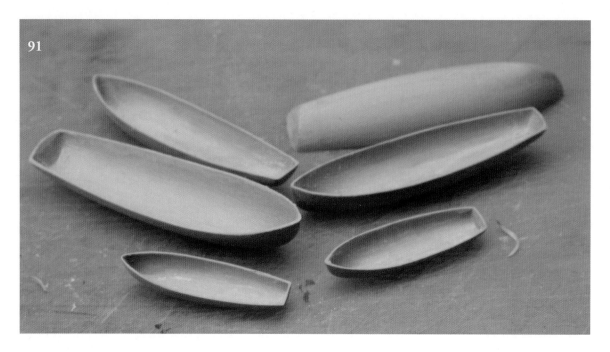

91.

Once the required numbers of castings have been taken they can be trimmed to size and thoroughly cleaned up to remove any traces of wax. I usually use an old stiff bristled paintbrush, starting out with white spirit and finishing up with hot water and detergent.

92.

Strips of boxwood have been cut to size for the keels and they have been glued to the hulls.

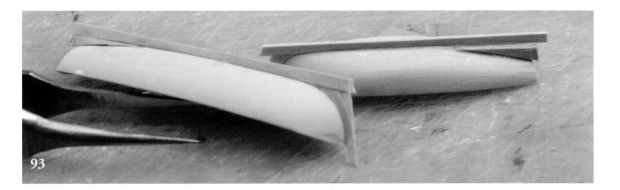

93.

Stems have been cut and fitted and at the stern wedges of wood inserted between the hull and the keel. As can be seen they are considerably wider than the keel.

94.

Using the burr shown in the photograph the blocks can now be shaped to blend with the curves of the hull.

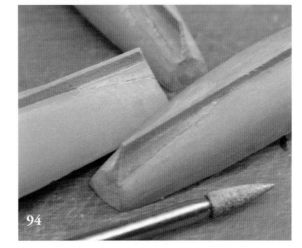

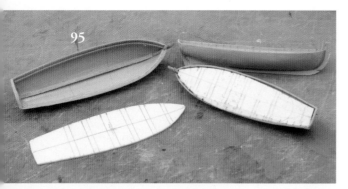

95.

Keelson and gunwale fitted and card jigs prepared, they have the position of all the thwarts marked on them. These positions are marked on either side of the boat.

96.

Now the frames can be fitted. Here I am positioning two between each thwart. They are cut from paper and glued in place with superglue.

97.

The outsides of the cutters have been planked with paper, a backboard added and paper boards fitted to the bottom of the boat.

98.

With the interiors finished they are painted with the airbrush. This gives a nice even finish and gets into all the awkward corners, under the bottom boards etc. Now thwarts are being prepared from boxwood.

99.

Gratings and thwarts in place and crudely shaped knees fitted where required; they will now be finally shaped with a diamond burr.

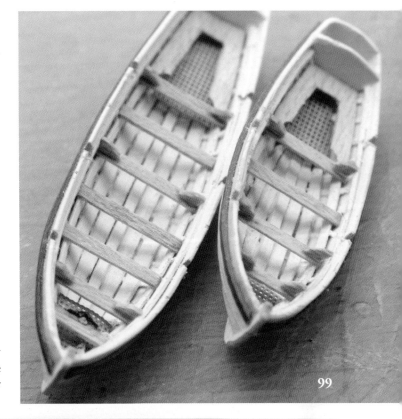

100.

One of the finished launches. Note the finished shape of the thwart knees, the heavy breasthook and the boxwood windlass.

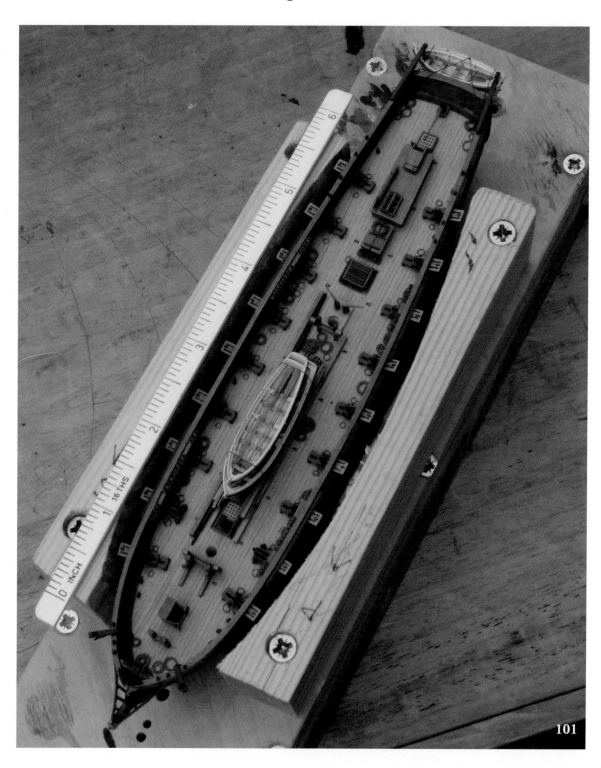

101

101.

Now, with all the fittings made, it is time to start assembly. However, before moving inboard it is a good idea to fit the gunport lids along with their lanyards and then engineer some sort of protection for them. The two pieces of wood shown here not only serve that purpose but are also invaluable hand rests while working on the decks. I have included a rule to give some idea of scale.

The following photographs are taken in close up and should give a good idea of the models prior to making a start on the rigging. One particular point of interest and one that many of you, particularly on this side of the pond, may have noticed is the absence of either windlass or capstan. Many of the American privateer schooners of this period were not fitted with either. With their large crews they were able to manhandle the anchors using a series of double or treble purchases, two for each cable. In practice one block would be nipped to the cable forward and the other to a ringbolt aft.

102

102.

The completed bow of the model with all the fittings in place including timberheads and a variety of cleats. Coils of rope have been glued to the decks where required and hanks fitted to all the pin rails.

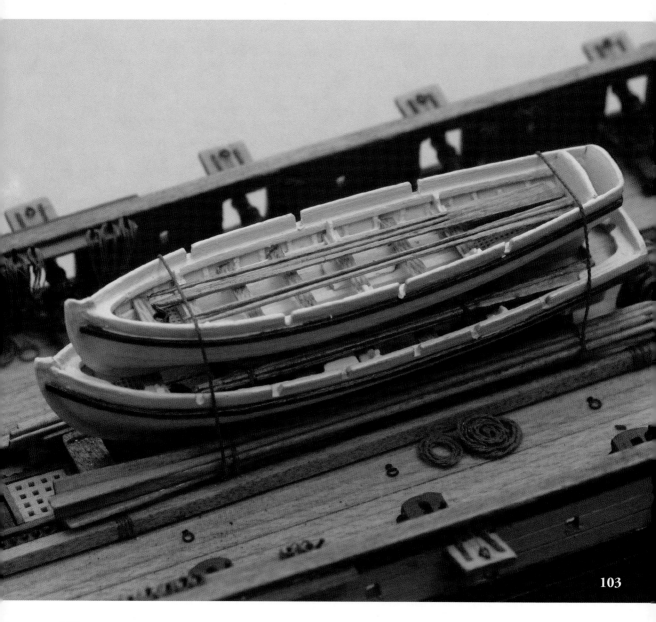

103

103.

Midships and the boats. The oars for the boats were brass etched, I had several sheets of a variety of fittings made up for me some years ago. Some have been useful but many, in my opinion, did not give as good a finish as is obtained by more traditional methods. Miniature oars, for instance, can be made from fine brass wire, the blades being beaten flat with a jeweller's hammer. Other points of interest here are the small-arms chest just under the bow of the launch and the storage of the sweeps, spare spars and timber. These are all fixed down to the deck both with glue and either twisted tails from the lashings (the sweeps), or, in the case of the spare spars and timber, holes drilled and copper wire pins inserted between strands of the lashings. These were then teased back into position. The ropes securing the boats also feed down and are glued in holes pre-drilled in the deck.

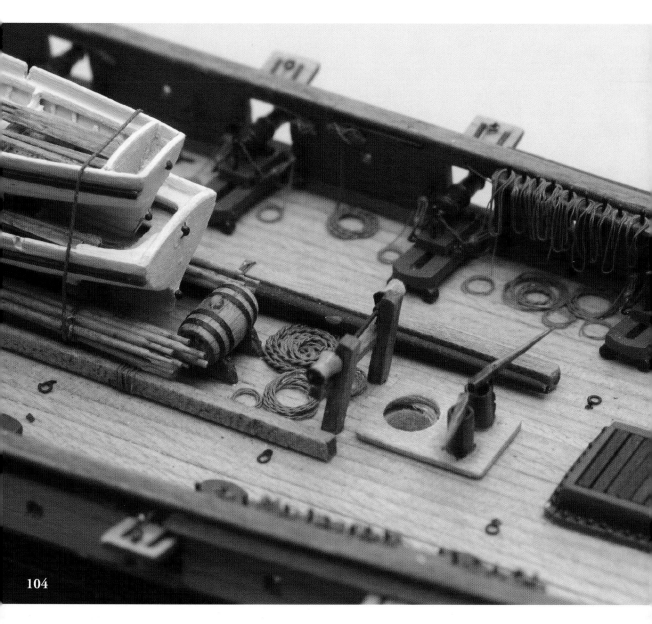

104.

104.

Of interest here are the pumps and drinking water barrel. This was turned from boxwood; individual staves were scored in with a knife, it was stained and had paper hoops fitted. Note also the shot in the garlands; these were tiny painted glass beads that were very kindly given to me a little while ago. Before that I made all my shot from Milliput, a most tedious job, particularly on a large vessel.

105.

Looking aft, giving a clearer view of the pumps and fire buckets with their rope handles. Just behind them are another pair of small-arms chests that I chose to fit. Also to be seen are the boarding pikes racked on top of the aft deckhouse.

106.

The stern of the schooner, looking down the stern companionway, and a good view of the second cutter with its attendant tackles.

∽ Carving a Sea ∽

At this stage, while the models are relatively easy to handle without damaging them, thought has to be given to their final display. In this instance the waterline model will be set in a carved wooden sea and the full-hull model mounted on two cradles.

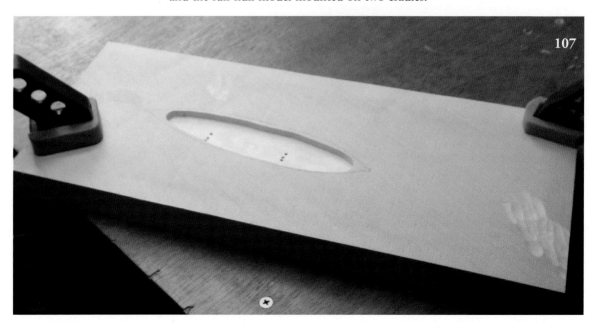

107.

A couple of years ago I managed to obtain some boards of Tupelo. This tree comes from the flood plains of the southern United States and is widely used by carvers there. It is readily available in the US but is less easy to obtain in Great Britain (See Materials and Tools, page 126). So far I have used it to carve several seas, and have rather mixed feelings about its qualities. It is quite unbelievably light, stable and tough, but will tear while being carved unless the tools are kept razor sharp. So steer clear unless you have the ability to keep tools at this pitch. But with the sharpest of tools it carves like a dream, in any direction either along or across the grain. In fact, it sometimes feels more like carving hard cheese than wood.

This photograph shows a board, planed and thicknessed, and with a recess routed to accept the hull. This was made slightly smaller than the waterline dimensions of the model to allow for final trimming to size. This is done by repeatedly offering

the hull up to the sea, marking in, and then carefully trimming the edge back little by little with either chisels and gouges, or a suitable burr in the Minicraft drill. If the ship is to be heeling to port or starboard then the recess will either have to be cut deeper on one side or, if the recess is of sufficient depth, a small batten of wood can be glued on one side of the recess. Note also the holes drilled to accept the screwed rods in the base of the hull; these also have to take into account the heel of the ship and are best drilled before cutting the recess, though as you can see if you look carefully I ended up re-drilling several times before I was happy with position and angle. There is quite a lot of trial and error in getting the ship to sit 'just right' in the board. It is quite important to continually try and visualise the ship with the sea carved and sails set. On the underside of the board two round recesses have been routed to allow washers and nuts to be fitted to the ends of the threaded rods fitted in the hull.

108.

The actual carving is done with a 'Flexcut' gouge. I have been using these excellent little tools for a while now; there are a whole range of interchangeable blades and they hold a very sharp edge. They are also small and handy when working at these small scales. Before making a start mark in the wave crests, and all the time while carving, keep in mind the wind direction and the appearance of the final picture you wish to create. When satisfied with the result the sea can be lightly sanded or rubbed over with some fine wire wool.

109.

The final job in the shaping of the sea is to add bow wave, wake and wave crests. The model has been wrapped in very thin polythene with as close a fit around the sides as possible, with short strips of adhesive tape to hold it in place. Next I prepared some Milliput epoxy putty and rolled out some thin strips, and these were pressed firmly in place around the top of the inside of the recess for the hull. These strips were then treated to a good warm-up with a hair dryer to soften the putty and then the model was pressed firmly into the recess and the washers and nuts fitted and tightened until the model was sitting at the correct water level both fore and aft. Finally, using a modelling tool, or a sharpened strip of boxwood, trim away the putty that will have oozed up the side of the hull and shape, from some fresh putty, the bow wave and other adjacent wave crests. When dry trim back the polythene so that the model can be removed before peeling away the remains of the polythene.

Sometimes models can be quite stubborn to remove, but a few gentle taps on the ends of the screwed rods usually does the trick.

The sea can now be given several coats of undercoat, I prefer something quite neutral like a mid-grey, as white can take several coats of enamel to cover completely. In between coats a gentle rub down with fine sandpaper or wire wool should be given. I paint my seas with Humbrol enamels, and spend quite a time mixing the exact colours and shades that I think I shall need. Then I just wade in, the darker shades go on first, even darker close to the hull, then before it can dry, lighter areas are blended in towards the tops of the waves, finally the crests are painted white. When dry it can be given a couple of coats of varnish. I personally do not think that it is a good idea to use gloss automatically. It works well on a glassy calm but where the wind whips across the waves and the tiny ripples produce a matting effect, then a satin finish seems appropriate.

∽ *Making Cradles* ∽

110.

Supports of some description now have to be provided for the other model, and many options are available, but I have chosen to make a pair of boxwood cradles.

The first step is to make a card jig for each of them, which is needed primarily to establish the angles of the hull at the relevant points and also the base of the cradle where it sits on the plinth.

110

111.

Using the templates, the angles are marked on some timber and the rough for each of the cradles drawn freehand. A tracing of each is then taken, turned over, and the second sides transferred to the wood.

111

112

112.

Cut to shape, but a little oversize, using the fretsaw.

113.

I have now set one of the cradles in a machine vice and am drilling through the centre to accommodate the threaded rod. If you are doing this job without these facilities, drill from each end with a very small drill bit, and then gradually enlarge the hole with successively larger bits.

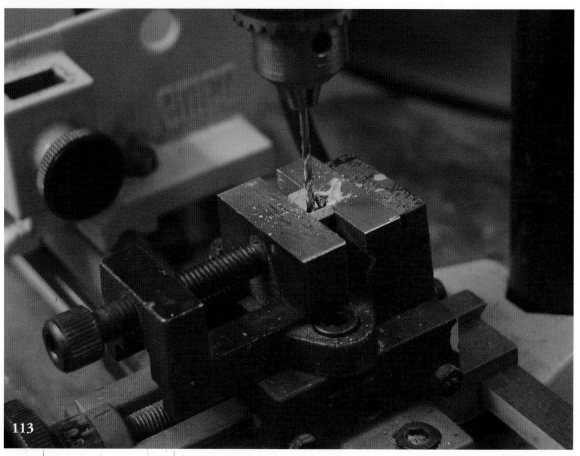

113

114.

Now each of the cradles can be threaded on its rod and offered up to the hull. The first job is the opening up of the slot for the keel; when this fits mark as shown on all sides of the cradle and then remove and trim or sand down to the lines.

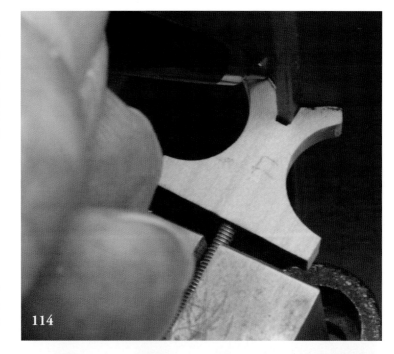

115.

When satisfied with the fit to the hull, check that they both sit flush and level on the plinth.

116.

Now check that the little ship is sitting upright. The dark rectangle to the right is actually the back of the handle of a little engineer's square. It is fixed, with double-sided tape, to the back of the large set square on which is marked a green grid, supporting it, and ensuring that it is upright. In the foreground is another set square lined up with the side of the plinth. Now it is possible to stand back from the model and see if any more adjustments are required.

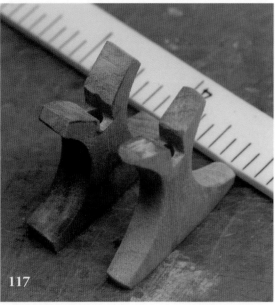

117.

When the fit is satisfactory they can be removed, and then trimmed and sanded to their final shape, ready for painting or staining.

Masts and Spars

I shall outline the basic techniques that I use both at this scale and at the smaller scale (1/384) to which I sometimes work. I would not, for instance, use thread at either of these smaller scales, but rather complete all the rigging with wire. For some models a masting and rigging plan needs to be prepared, but with his subject all the information can be gleaned from the extant plans.

The first job is to prepare some timber for the masts and spars. I used lemonwood but I think box works just as well. I ran off enough for all the masts and spars on the Preac saw, initially just as square stuff, but some was planed to octagonal section and then finished round on the lathe.

118.

I should explain that 'lathe' here is the Minicraft drill that I have semi-permanently mounted on the right-hand side of my work bench. It is handy for all sorts of small turning jobs and will cope with all these tiny masts and spars without the need to keep going next door to my Unimat lathe.

In practice one end of the timber is placed in the chuck and the other end sanded round with the disc sander, while steadying the spar with the other hand. This can then be reversed and the other end treated similarly. Note the dust extraction nozzle on its flexible tube.

119.

The lower masts can be sanded to the correct dimensions, using the disc sander, but should be finished with a sanding board made from wood or card with some fine sandpaper fixed to it with double-sided tape. A selection of these boards in different sizes and grades is invaluable for this work. The mastheads are cut square with a knife and then cleaned up with a file; they will be finished to their final dimensions later.

120.

The spars are first planed octagonal before mounting them in the lathe and sanding to shape one end at a time with the rotary sander and boards, the central section being left octagonal.

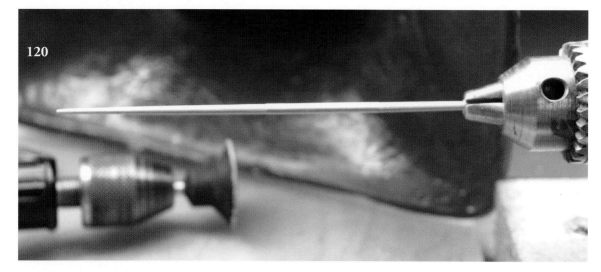

121.

The topmasts were made from square stuff, made over-long and turned round at the ends so they can be fitted centrally in the chuck. The centres were then shaved to an octagonal section with a sharp knife and finished round on the lathe.

122.

The topgallant masts were turned, including their trucks, in the same manner. The diamond burr in the foreground is very useful for cutting the underside of the trucks.

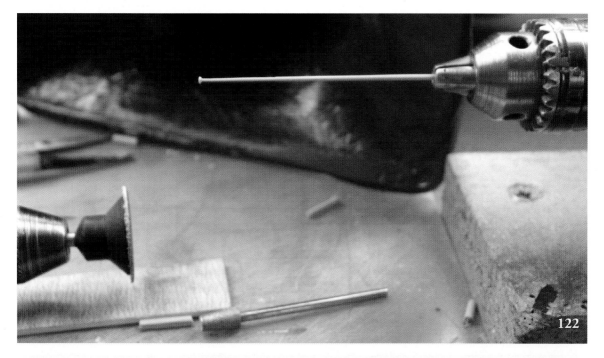

123.

124.

A shoulder has been cut to accept the cheeks, which are shown here at different stages of completion. To the back they are cut roughly to size and fitted, and in the foreground sanded to final size and shape. At about this stage I like to stain all the round sections of the masts and spars; all those areas in fact that will not be finally painted black. I use a mixture of burnt sienna and raw umber artists' oil colour, preferably of the quick-drying variety which is now available. I will mix this with a little satin finish polyurethane varnish and white spirit, and then after brushing it on the spar wipe it to a smooth finish with the tip of a finger.

To make the jaws for the gaffs the ends of the spars are planed off on either side, and roughly shaped, oversize jaws glued in place. Then, first with a drill, and then using a fine burr or stone, the gape of the jaws is opened up to the diameter of the mast.

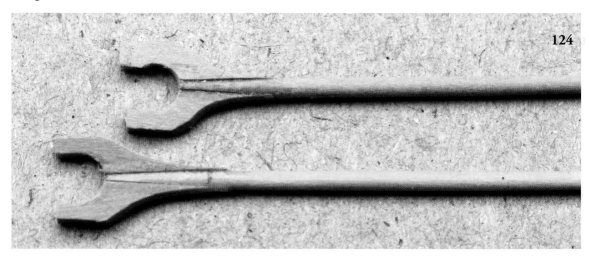

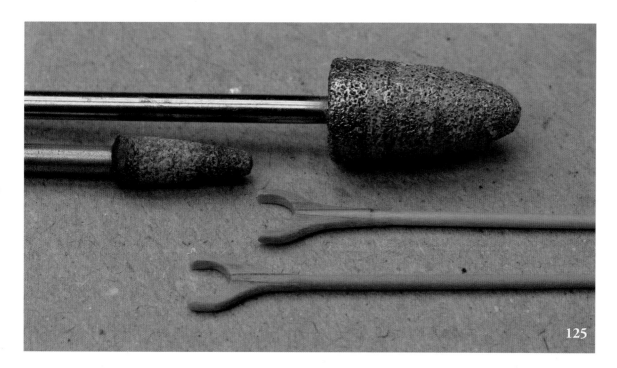

125.

They can then be finally shaped, again using a variety of stones and burrs.

126.

The top for *Neufchatel* is built up, rather unusually, from open spaced battens, making it a little more difficult to make than a planked one. The first job is to prepare and glue strips of boxwood to a sheet of stiff card for the crosstrees, but only at their ends. The three strips of box at the front will form the crosstrees and, although the battens will be glued to all four, the rearmost one is simply for temporary support and will ultimately be cut away. The battens themselves were cut from some scraps of wood shaving mounted on paper left over from another job, which explains why some are black and others natural. Enough were cut and mounted on the crosstrees for the tops of both models.

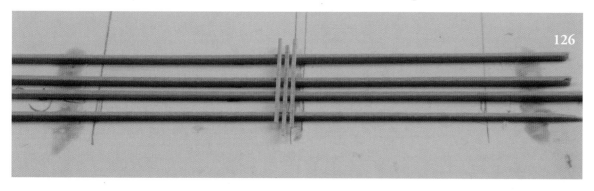

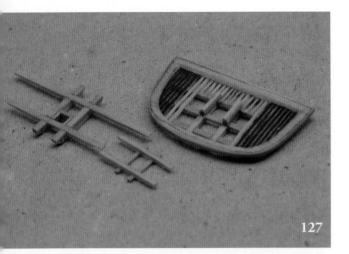

127

127.

Next, the wooden rim was carefully cut from a plane shaving and glued to the battens while these were still mounted on the card. When dry the whole ensemble can be removed, turned over and the unwanted battens around, and in the centre of, the top carefully cut away. Now the trestletrees are made, with slots cut or filed out to fit over the crosstrees. They are, of course, fitted from below, something not entirely clear in this photograph because I have subsequently fitted strips of shaving over the forward section of the trestletrees. At this stage it is important to check for fit over the masthead, and once this is done the bolsters can be added.

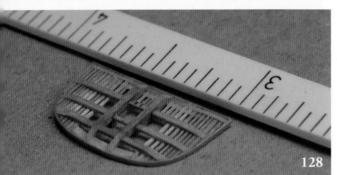

128

128.

Initially, using the disc sander and then a sanding board, the ends of the cross- and trestletrees were tapered. Finally, a thin paper rim was fitted all around the edge of the top. Before painting and fitting to the mast, holes need to be drilled for the topmast shrouds and a slot cut for the foreyard sling.

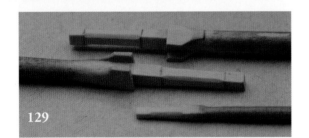

129

129.

Before fitting the tops, all the mastheads are carefully finished to their final dimensions and the edges chamfered to an octagonal section.

130

130.

Now the tops can be glued in place and wire rigging, of the correct diameter for the lower and topmast shrouds, wound around the masthead to represent the upper ends of the shrouds.

131.

I always used to make mastcaps from boxwood for all my models, but recently, on small models, I have been constructing some of them *in situ* from card and paper. As I am building two models I can demonstrate both methods here, so first of all here is the card method. This is made feasible by the use of the ultra-thin superglues now available from model shops and suppliers. However, all the actual construction of the top is done using a thick and tacky superglue that will obviously set quickly and not soak into the card.

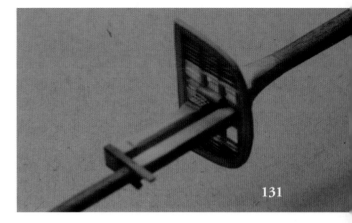

131

The first stage in the process is to glue a piece of card to the very top front edge of the lower masthead. In size this should be the depth of the cap and the width of the masthead. Now fit the topmast in its hole in the top and offer it up to the card; hold in place while checking against the plans to see if the angles of both masts are correct. If they are not then either trim the card back a little or add another layer of paper or card. When satisfied, glue the topmast in place, both to the top and the card. If you want to make a really strong fixing then drill through both masts and the card spacer with a size 80 or similar drill and fit a wire pin. The rest of the top can now be assembled as shown, using card of the correct thickness. When all four sides have been fitted the whole cap is liberally treated with the thin superglue, applied very carefully with a wire so that it does not get on to the areas of exposed mast. The card will soak up this glue like blotting paper, turning it into a very tough fibre-board that can be sanded and drilled with ease.

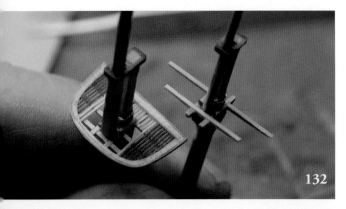

132.

The finished caps, sanded to their final shape.

133.

A cap made from boxwood; the method should be largely self-explanatory. The cap should first of all be made over-large as shown on the right of the picture, before trimming to final size. Care is required to ensure that the round hole for the topmast and square one for the masthead are exactly the right distance apart.

134.

The bowsprit, jib-boom and flying jib-boom were all turned in exactly the same manner as the other spars, but bowsprit and jib-boom were left a little oversize at their inboard ends to allow for planing them to an octagonal section. The bowsprit was treated in the same way at its tip, though in his case to enable it to be planed square. A tenon was cut at an angle on the inboard end of the bowsprit to fit the gap between the fore bitts and sit flush with the deck. A recess was then cut to accept the bees which were made from ⅟₆₄in ply, and a saddle for the spritsail yard made from paper and wire.

To assemble the bowsprit and jib-boom I used the same card technique to construct the cap as was used on the masts, with a small rectangle of card used for the jib-boom saddle where a second pin was fitted through both spars. The job was then completed by fitting a paper strap around both to represent what appears to be a metal strap on the plans, rather than a rope lashing. The flying jib-boom irons were formed by winding some fine wire around and between both spars in a figure-of-eight motion for three or four turns, bedding them tightly together and finally securing with a little superglue. They were subsequently further built up with woodworking adhesive and painted. One detail I accidentally omitted to fit at this stage was the traveller for the jib-stay. See photograph 169.

135.

The masts and bowsprit assembled and painted. I chose to use an airbrush for this job mainly because of the fine slats of the foretop, but careful hand-painting would serve just as well.

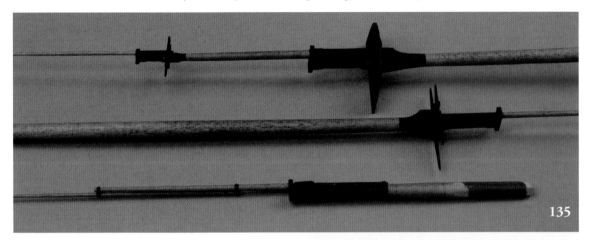

136.

Now the spars need to be brought to the same degree of finish. Both they and the booms and gaffs have been fitted with the necessary ironwork, and copper wire inserted in pre-drilled holes; these will be used to give a secure fixing to the mast. I have also inserted a wire pin in the centre of the fore yard for the same reason, but have not extended the same treatment to the upper yards as it would weaken such small items.

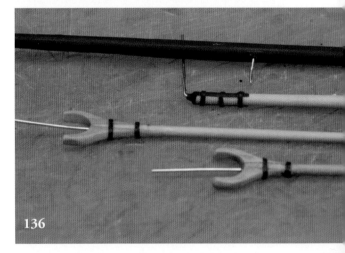

137.

A couple of other mast fittings can be made at this stage and then set aside till required. The first are the mast coats, and these I chose to turn. This can be done on a lathe or, as is demonstrated here, in the chuck of the little drill I keep fixed to my bench. A length of boxwood dowel is drilled to the diameter of the mast with successively larger bits in a Minicraft drill, both drills revolving. A little practice may be required to keep the drill centred and in line with the dowel, but it is actually easier than it looks.

138.

Now the coat can be sanded and parted off with either a sharp blade or a razor saw. It may help to insert the shank of the drill while doing this; it is a delicate operation and care is needed.

139.

Secondly, the mast hoops should be prepared in advance, and a mental note made not to fit any lower mast fittings like spider bands or goose neck for the boom until they have been threaded on to the mast. I speak from experience.

I have seen these bands made very successfully from painted wire but I have always used the following method. Dowel of a slightly greater diameter than the mast is firstly prepared and lightly waxed. Then a strip of ordinary brown gumstrip is wound once around the dowel before moistening the remainder and making another couple of turns. When dry the surplus paper is trimmed away.

140.

Then individual hoops are cut from the paper tube by placing the knife blade on top of it and carefully rolling the tube forward with the blade, taking great care to cut just a hoop's width from the end. The individual hoops are now picked up with tweezers and dipped in some of the thin superglue on a piece of glass, then touched to some absorbent paper to remove any surplus and placed on some non-absorbent paper to dry. This method produces strong and realistic hoops: no other treatment is required. Now the yards and spars can be set aside while rigging material and blocks are prepared.

⌒ *Block Making* ⌒

141.

141.

At a larger scale I usually make the blocks from wood, but it is not a very viable method for a small vessel at this scale. I also make them from Milliput, an epoxy putty, that works reasonably well. A long thin sausage of Milliput is rolled out to the required diameter and is then allowed to partially set. It is then slightly flattened and individual blocks are sliced from it. They are stropped by gluing a length of wire to one side, which when dry is bent to a dog's leg to line up with the centre of the block; a fine groove is then filed on either edge to suggest the sheave openings. One of the disadvantages of this method is catching the Milliput at just the right degree of set for rolling and cutting, which also, of course, means that there is quite a limited time for carrying out these tasks.

On the *Neufchatel* models I made the blocks with punched ovals of card. I have in the past bought various sets of punches of varying degrees of uselessness, some of which were redeemable by re-turning on the lathe, but I have yet to find any quality punches small enough for this sort of work.

Provided you have access to a lathe they are very easy to make. For many years I used punches made from 4- and 6in nails. The three on the right of the picture above are examples of these, and they did sterling service though they needed regular sharpening; finally I decided to make some from silver steel. The process is quite straightforward. A suitable length of steel rod is fitted in the lathe chuck and a drill of the required size in the tailstock. The rod is then drilled, turned, removed from the lathe and a section of the shaft ground away to allow access to the drilled hole a little way up the shaft. A blowtorch is then used to heat the tips to a bright cherry-red before plunging them into a tin of engine oil to temper them. If they are to be used for making blocks then at the cherry-red stage they are taken to the anvil (the top of a steel vice in my case) and the end of the punch is gently beaten on two sides until the required profile is achieved; they are then reheated and plunged. The tips are finally sharpened and polished on a leather wheel. The seven punches on the right have been shaped for block making.

142.

I use the end grain of a block of boxwood while punching, with the paper or card being used held in place with a little Sellotape. Several ovals at a time can be punched before expelling with the little wire ejector.

143.

It would be quite impossible to demonstrate making one of the 7in blocks being punched in the previous photograph, so I am making a 24in block here (larger than any on *Neufchatel*). A length of suitable wire rigging has been dipped in white glue and offered up to one of the ovals.

144.

When dry, more white glue is brushed on to the wire and it is turned over and placed over the second oval. If a double block is required a short strip of wire is added to one face and the process repeated. A little more glue can then be used to close the ends of the block. Finally, as with the mast hoops, each block is treated with thin superglue.

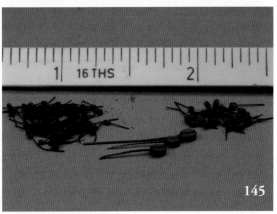

145.

When a batch of blocks is completed they are mounted in modelling clay on a strip of wood and painted black. I used an airbrush, but would hand-paint if there were only a few of them. Then both sides are painted brown, leaving a black centreline for the strop. It sounds rather fiddly painting blocks this way, but when you get into the swing of it two little brush strokes deal with each side and the job gets done surprisingly quickly. The large blocks in the foreground are 24in, those on the left 7in and those on the right 10in.

146.

I have always used copper wire for rigging miniature models. I have experimented with other materials but have found them generally unsatisfactory. The majority of my stock is tinned copper bought many years ago from Ormiston Wire Ltd (See Materials and Tools, page 126). The finest has a diameter of 0.080mm, and the remaining seven spools are successively larger. The one non-tinned wire I use is from a spool of very thin ordinary copper wire that I use for the finest ropes.

146

147.

For 1½in and 2in ropes I use a single strand of the two finest wires, but for all other sizes two or three strands of wire need to be wound together. This is easily accomplished with either a lathe or mounted drill. The requisite number of strands are removed from the spool and given a slight stretch to straighten them, and the ends then inserted in the chuck, doubled over a couple of times, and given a few twists; this gives the chuck something to bite on. Now hold the other ends taut and run the drill until the rope is satisfactorily formed, then give it another slight stretch before removing it from the drill. I show only a short length of rope being wound here; I would normally make lengths of at least 3ft, being limited only by the spread of my hands from the end of the wire to the switch on the drill.

147

148

148.

I paint the rigging with matt Humbrol enamels, No 29 (dark earth) for the running rigging and a very dark brown of my own mixing for the standing rigging. It is applied in the following way. A long piece of hardboard, used specifically for the purpose, is placed on the bench and a brush full of paint puddled on it about a foot from the edge. A length of rigging is laid along the board and steadily drawn through the puddle and under the brush, allowing the wire to drag across the surface of the board a short distance to remove any surplus paint. It then needs to be hung up to dry. I find double-sided tape along the edge of a convenient shelf to be the answer to this.

149.

When the rigging is painted it needs to be stored. I have a set of homemade drawers, two of which are used for this purpose. One of them has a strip of plasticine at either end into which lengths of rigging are embedded, and the other has a series of channels and is primarily used for shorter lengths, offcuts and less frequently used sizes. The channels were made by scoring a sheet of card and then folding it concertina fashion to form the individual dividers, and then applying a little glue where necessary.

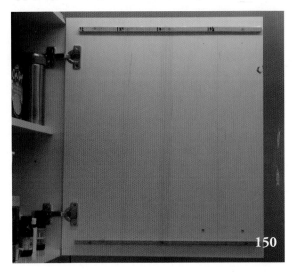

150.

Another solution (I use it as backup, particularly when rigging a larger vessel) is to make use of the inside of a cupboard door. Two battens of wood are fitted top and bottom and double-sided tape applied to them.

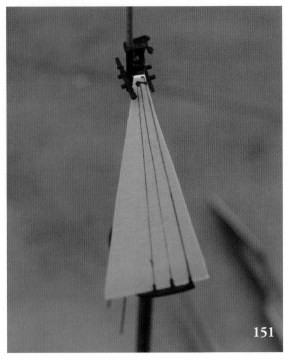

151.

With masts and spars made and blocks and rigging material prepared I have now returned to the job of detailing the masts. To keep things clearer I shall be showing the assembling of the bare-spars model, followed by notes and photographs showing preparation and fitting of sails as used on the waterline model.

All the shrouds fitted with ratlines on my miniature models are prepared in the same way. However, those for the topmasts, and on some models the topgallant masts, are prepared and fitted before the masts are finally glued in place on the model. The lower shrouds are prepared at a later stage, the reasons for which will become clear in due course.

The method I use for making these is as follows. First I use a little machine vice to secure the mast in an upright position, and then cut out a triangle of card that will sit squarely along the edge of the maintop and between the topmast crosstrees. I now mark the base of the card where the holes have been drilled for the shrouds and the top of the card in line with the topmast head. The card is then removed and the shrouds drawn in as shown in this photograph.

152.

The card has been removed and laid on top of another piece of card, carefully lining up the bases of both pieces of card. A knife or scalpel is then used to mark through both pieces at either end of the shrouds, so marking exactly the layout on the card beneath. This is then turned over and the knife cuts joined up to give a mirror image of the original. We now have a plan for both port and starboard topmast shrouds.

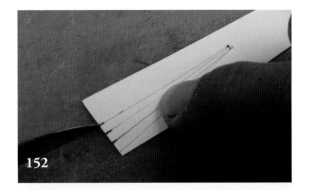

152

153.

I have quite a collection of jigs that I use for the preparation of shroud assemblies. These two will fit the bill admirably for *Neufchatel,* they can be made from any stable board about ¼in-½in thick, they are fitted with a strip of wood top and bottom, wide enough to give a raised edge of about ⅛in on either side. Strips of paper marked at 15in scale divisions are then glued to either edge and on both sides of the jig; 2mm is about right for this scale. I mark out a fairly large area using a ruler and set square and then trim strips off when required.

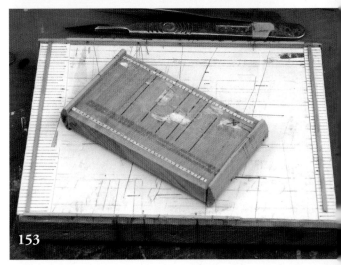

153

154.

The two shroud plans are now glued either side of the jig, immediately opposite one another. Note the black guide lines on the jig, it is important that the base of the card plan is parallel with one of these; this will ensure that the ratlines run parallel with the maintop and the waterline. Obviously this is not always true for lower shrouds, as channels are not always horizontal and ratlines should be. This difference then has to be allowed for.

154

155.

Before starting to wind the shrouds the four edges of the jig have strips of double-sided tape attached to them, and the backing tape at top and bottom removed. Now a length of 4in wire is wound and a knot tied in one end. This is inserted in a slot cut with a razor saw in the base of the jig and pulled tight.

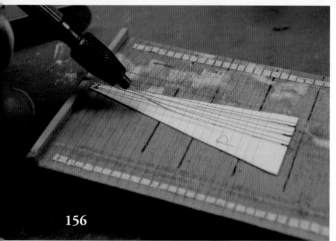

156.

The winding of shrouds and ratlines is quite straight-forward; the shrouds go on first, lining them up with the plans on each side of the jig. The backing is then removed from the tape along the sides and the ratlines are wound over the top of them, lining them up with the marks on the paper strips. When completed, superglue is run along each shroud, applied with a fine wire.

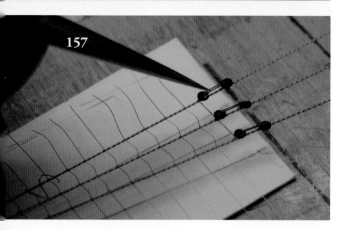

157.

Now the ratlines can be cut through either side of the shrouds, and a downwards sag carefully put on each between the shrouds. Next, discs of paper are punched to represent the deadeyes and glued in place. The upper one should be set slightly off-centre to allow for the later fitting of the turned-in end of the shroud. Finally, two of the lengths of lanyard are glued in place, the centre and right-hand ones on each deadeye.

158.

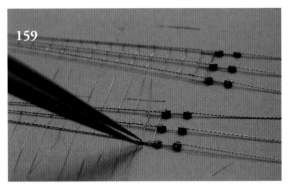

159.

I have cut back the tip of a No 11a scalpel blade to allow me to reach between shroud and lanyard and cut away the section of shroud between the deadeyes.

The shrouds are then turned over and short lengths of wire glued in place to represent their turned-in ends, and the ratlines trimmed right back to the outside shrouds. The work is then completed by building up the deadeyes flush with the shrouds using white glue and then fitting the remaining lanyard lengths. Finally, all but the lanyards are given a coat of dark brown paint. I did this with several thin coats applied with a brush as it hardly seemed worth setting up the airbrush for two such simple assemblies.

160.

161.

Bobstays and bowsprit shrouds are next made up, but not being formed on a jig each one can be constructed in two parts, obviating the removal of the section between the deadeyes. Also each deadeye was formed from two paper discs, one either side of the wires.

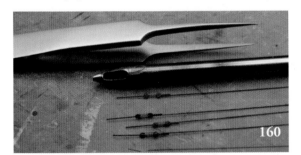

Before fitting the spider bands the mast hoops must be threaded on to the mast.

This photograph shows the paper spider band fitted to the mast. It has been drilled to take the lugs for the belaying pins. In the foreground a length of wire is being twisted round a belaying pin, it can then be trimmed and glued into one of the holes. Just above it can be seen the mast band carrying the saddle for the boom gooseneck. I made the saddle from a piece of very fine tubing produced by stretching an empty refill from a ballpoint pen after softening it in a candle flame. This was bound to the mast with some fine wire to produce the mast band and a strong anchorage for the saddle. The wire was treated with a couple of coats of superglue to disguise the individual strands and painted. I really do not know why I am telling you this because when it came to fitting the boom I decided to straighten the gooseneck and drill a hole in the mast immediately above the band. It made a more secure fixing and was visually virtually identical. However, if at some time in the future you are in need of some very fine tubing, spacers or washers, try a ballpoint refill.

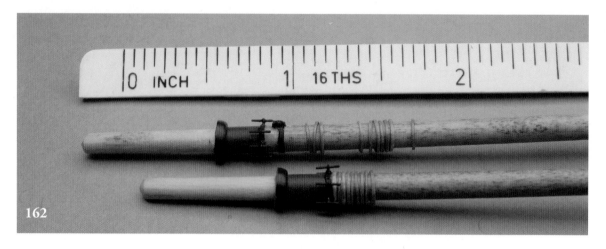

162.

The lower end of the masts completed. A dummy bolt has been fitted from the base of the boom saddle, and the mast coats glued in place while *in situ* on the model to ensure a tight fit to the deck.

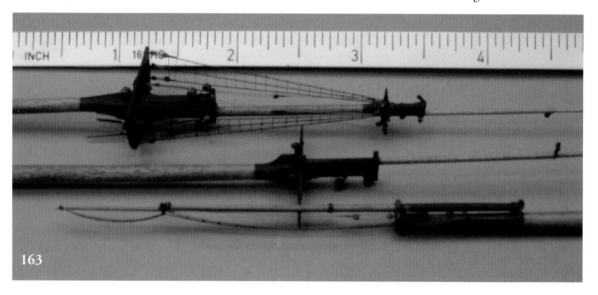

163.

Now the following fittings can be added to the masts and bowsprit. Working down from the top of the foremast are blocks for the flying jib halyard, main topgallant braces, topsail yard lifts, outer jib halyard, fore yard lifts, main topmast stay, gaff peak and throat halyards, the fore topsail halyard, pendants of tackles and the blocks under the fore top for the spritsail yard braces and fore yard buntlines. The topsail reef tackles can also be made up and fitted along with the trusses and sling for the fore yard.

Finally, the fore topmast shrouds are glued in place.

On the mainmast, again working downwards, blocks are fitted for the fore topgallant brace, fore topsail yard brace, gaff peak halyard, boom topping lift, pendants of tackle and gaff throat halyard.

On the bowsprit assembly, working inboard from the tip of the jib-boom, footropes are fitted back to the bowsprit cap. The jib stay outhaul is fitted under the jib-boom, and blocks are in place for the topgallant, topsail and foresail bowlines.

164.

There are three other fittings that can be added to the model before embarking on the final rigging. I purposely left them till this late stage as they would be easily damaged if accidentally snagged while working on the hull. They are the anchors, boomkins, and tackles for the mainstays. The fitting of anchors and boomkins should need no further explanation than that given in the photograph; however, a little more information about the mainstay tackles is necessary. These ropes would be long enough to allow one of them to be slackened off sufficiently for the fore gaff sail to be swung out to port or starboard. This feature can be seen quite clearly in the photographs of the finished waterline model.

165.

The boom and both gaffs have been fitted to the masts. This should initially be done while in place on the model to ensure they are set at the correct angle. They can then be fitted in a vice or block of wood and the peak and throat halyards and boom topping lifts fitted.

166.

Also fitted at this stage were the gaff parrel beads made from some of the tiny glass beads used for the shot.

167.

Now the bowsprit is finally glued in place and will be rigged before fitting the masts. The first item to be added is the lower end of the forestay. The wire was first of all bent round a drill shank and bound in place with a fine wire whipping. The deadeyes were then formed by gluing two punched discs of paper either side of the circle of wire. Plenty of superglue was used to allow it to fill the intervening space.

167

168.

After the forestay collar the gammoning, bowsprit shrouds and bobstays are added. Then comes the dolphin striker (pre-drilled with four holes), through which are threaded the jib-boom and flying jib-boom martingale stays and the fore royal and fore topgallant stays, all set up with single blocks to the bulwarks either side of the bowsprit. Next, from their respective blocks to the fore pin rail, via holes drilled in the fairleads at the bow, bowlines are fitted for the fore course, topsail and topgallant, as well as the spritsail lifts and the jib outhaul.

When fitting the stays to the end of the spars I bind them in place with the finest of wire taken once round the spar and shroud and tied with a half hitch. The shroud can then be pulled taut and a spot of glue applied, the end of the shroud trimmed, and a couple more turns of the wire given before finishing off.

169.

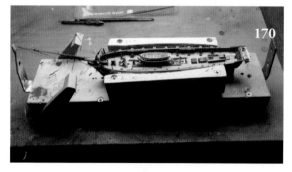

170.

One detail I have now to fit is the traveller for the jibstay; this was fiddly work because I had to work around all the rigging that was now in place. It consists of a wire hoop with another smaller loop at the top to which the stay will be attached and the short length of outhaul from sheave to traveller. If you refer back to photographs 132 and 133 you will see how much easier it would have been to make and then fit the traveller at that stage.

As the work of rigging the model proceeds I add to the protective structure around it. Here I have fixed a bracket at either end to protect the flying jib-boom and boom, once it has been added, and have made a couple of wooden and card brackets to protect the spritsail yard.

171.

The jib-boom and flying jib-boom guys are next made up with their tackles and fitted, first inserting the ends in holes drilled in the catheads, then gluing them to the spritsail yard before taking them to the ends of their respective booms.

172.

Now the masts can be permanently glued in place, taking care that they are accurately positioned by checking from above and from bow and stern. When they are satisfactory the fore-and-aft stays are added, all except for the fore royal and main topgallant stays, These will be among the final items of rigging to be fitted due to their vulnerability, particularly when fitting the upper yard parrels.

The lower stays are installed as shown in the photograph, roughly shaped like the wire held in the foreground before feeding it around the masthead and drawing the two strands together with a whipping of fine wire. The remaining wire end is then cut away and white glue used to build a mouse around the whipping.

173.

The fore-and-aft stays in place along with the running rigging from all the blocks previously fitted to the masts down to the various pin rails.

174.

A close-up of the ropes brought down to the spider band and fore pin rails.

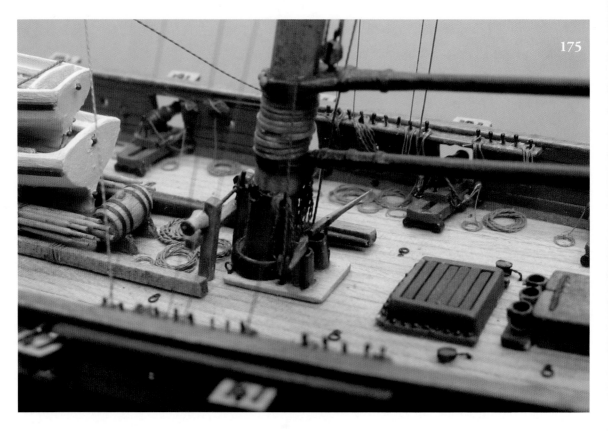

175.

The main spider band and rails.

176.

The stern, depicting the lashing I have fitted round the gaff, the boom sheets and the guy pendants.

177.

The lower shrouds are next prepared using exactly the same method as was used for the topmast shrouds, see photographs 149-157.

178.

When the shrouds had been completed and trimmed to fit between masthead and channels, I put a whipping of fine wire around all three shrouds as near the top as possible and then threaded a length of wire around the middle shroud, bringing both ends up in front of the whipping and gluing it in place with a spot of superglue.

179.

Notches are now cut in the edge of the channels and the shrouds glued in place, taking care that the upper ends of the shrouds are exactly lined up with the masthead.

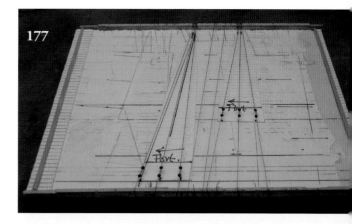

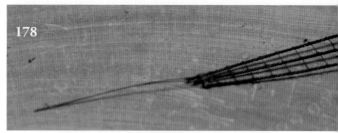

180.

The two lengths of wire attached to the top of the shrouds are now taken across the top, beneath the stay collars and are tied together in a half hitch before being drawn firmly but very gently tight. All can now be glued before trimming off the loose ends, and more superglue applied around the very top of the shrouds.

181.

The foremast futtock shrouds and lanyards are the next item to be fitted, followed by the ropes from the blocks under the top down to the pin rails. When fitting ropes such as these I cut them exactly to length before gluing them to the block. The lower end is then manoeuvred into its place on the pin rail. I usually find that this is most easily accomplished working from the opposite side of the ship with a thin boxwood push-stick with a flattened end and with a V cut in it. Then you have to reach through to apply a spot of superglue with a length of wire. It is fiddly work that becomes more difficult as the model progresses, and anyone who can complete the rigging of a model of this type without doing at least some damage to previously fitted rigging is a better man than I.

Before moving on with the assembly, the following items of rigging need to be prepared: the fore and main topmast and topgallant backstays, the fore royal backstays, the fore and main topsail halyards and the section of boom topping lift with its tackle from the blocks at the masthead down to the channels. The backstays are made up as previously described and the halyards in similar fashion by gluing all the ropes to one side of the blocks before fitting the other. The blocks can then be painted as shown earlier in photograph 143.

182.

When completed and painted the stays and halyards can be fitted. This photograph of the main masthead shows the remaining section of the boom topping lifts glued to their blocks and also shows how the wires used to draw in the shrouds close in to the top have blended in beneath the mainstay collar.

I find the best way to secure the backstays in place is to first glue the lower ends in their notches in the channels or the holes drilled in the rails (depending which stays are being fitted) and then loosely tie opposing backstays and the relevant masthead together with a loop of fine wire, again using a half hitch. Keeping the stays taut, the half hitch is pulled tight and a spot of glue applied. When the glue has set all the loose ends are removed.

183.

Capping rails and chain plates cut from black paper and then treated with superglue. The bolts for the chain plates are formed from dots of white glue applied with the tip of a fine brush.

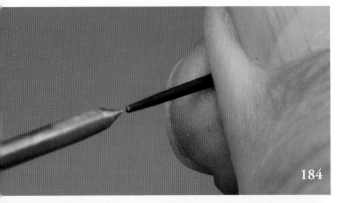

184.

With the masts in place and partially rigged it is now time to return to the yards. This photograph shows the ends of the fore yard being drilled to receive the boom irons; a job that is best got out the way while it is easy to grip the yard firmly without causing damage to the delicate fittings soon to be added to it.

185.

A very fine twist drill could be used to drill the yardarm ends, but a home-made drill with more rigidity and a sharp point makes the job much easier. The drill bit being used in the previous photograph and in many others throughout the book was made in the following way. An old drill bit was mounted in a Minicraft tool and offered up to a small grind wheel as shown, with both in motion. When the desired length and diameter of the tip is achieved the drill is stopped and the tip lightly touched to the wheel, at an angle, on three sides to provide a sharp three-sided cutting tip.

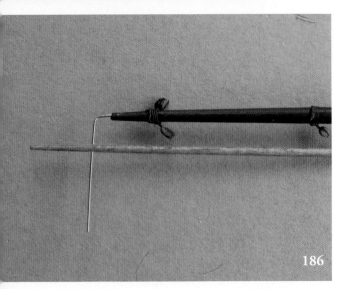

186.

Before fitting the boom irons, strops of wire rigging are glued in place around the yard for the various blocks and tackles to be fitted, and then holes drilled to receive them, alongside or between the strops. Here lift, brace and leech-line blocks can be seen glued in place. Wire for the shanks of the irons can now be glued in the holes in the ends of the yards and bent to a right angle. The same drill is used to drill through the stunsail booms; these are now fitted and glued, a lashing put round the inboard end of the spar and the surplus wire trimmed off.

187.

The boom irons are completed with the addition of paper hoops. A second iron will be needed a third of the boom's length from the end.

188.

The yards with most of their fittings; they are now ready for adding to the model. From the top they are the fore topgallant, main topmast, fore topmast and fore yard. Beneath them are the two lower stunsail booms. As these yards are for the model with bare spars, the fore royal yard and main topgallant yard are omitted; they would only have been crossed when in use and would have been set flying (without either braces or lifts).

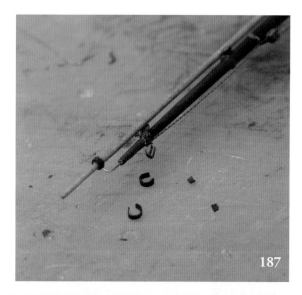

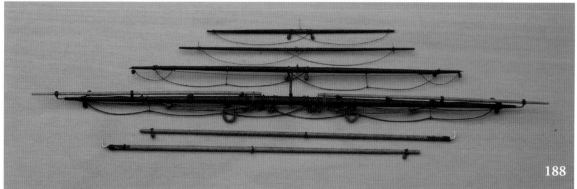

189.

The first of these spars to be fitted are the lower stunsail booms. Two holes are drilled in the channels and a wire bracket fitted; they can then be glued and lashed in place.

190.

Before finally fixing it to the model, the fore yard was fitted with strops for the trusses and sling; the footropes were also added along with the yard arm tackles. These and their coiled falls have been made up beneath the yard. The yard was then fitted to the model by the wire pin (see photograph 134) and the parrel fitted by threading the rope twice round the mast and once round the yard either side of the sling. This is fiddly and frequently frustrating work and patience is required. I always think that the time spent on some of these quite insignificant items is out of all proportion to the final result. Next, the lifts, buntlines and leech-lines are taken from the blocks on the yard to their respective blocks on the mast or under the tops, and the clue lines and sheets taken down to deck. The three components of each bowline were threaded under the stunsail boom and tacked in place before taking the top end around the

yard to meet itself on the fore side. These and other items of running rigging to the sails are tied off at convenient points on a spar or at a block, and may be omitted completely on a model such as this one.

This is also a good time to rig the spritsail yard braces, from the forestay collar to the blocks on the yard and back to the blocks under the top.

191.

Several feet beneath the fore yard can be seen the blocks for the cluelines, sheets and tacks. Before fitting these to the yard, or rather slinging them beneath it, they were made up as shown and the cluelines used to attach them to the yard. Then the sheets and tacks can be rigged to their sheaves or blocks.

192.

The fore topsail yard with the lifts, halyard and bowlines in place. Notice also in the bottom right-hand corner the cluelines whipped to the sheets in the absence of a sail.

193

193.

The fore topgallant yard with parrel, halyard, lifts and bowlines rigged. The cluelines have been fitted in the same manner as those for the topsail. The two ropes pointing to the top left-hand corner of the picture are the topgallant shrouds in the process of being fitted, they have been glued to shrouds and crosstrees and will now be angled in towards the mast, trimmed and glued in place.

194.

The main topmast yard rigged following the same sequence as the fore yards.

With the bulk of the rigging completed the vulnerable fore royal and main topgallant stays can be fitted and a Stars and Stripes (painted with acrylics on tissue paper) fitted to the mainmast . . .

195.

. . . and a pennant to the fore. All that now needs doing is to fit the remaining braces to the yards and the rigging is completed. I have not shown this last procedure in detail as it is very straightforward and clearly shown on the plans and in the final photographs.

196

196.

For those wanting to depict a waterline model under sail there are still the sails to be made and set on the masts and spars. The first job is to prepare ample sailcloth for the model with enough to spare for a few accidents. I use some quite fine tissue paper for this and tape it out over a completely flat surface like a sheet of glass. Then, using double-sided tape, a long steel rule is fixed to the glass at the bottom of the sheet. A ruler marked in millimeters is laid against the steel one and a set square used to mark in the individual cloths with a very sharp 4H pencil. On a full-scale ship these would normally be 24in wide, so I mark them 3mm apart, which, allowing for the overlap at the seams, would seem to be about right. Then the whole process is repeated on the other side of the paper, taking great care that the pencil lines are exactly in line with the original ones. The sheet of tissue is next taped over a wooden frame so both sides are exposed and is airbrushed on both sides with a very dilute mix of acrylic paint, matt medium and water. The finish I try to achieve is a slightly creamy off-white. This treatment will not only colour the tissue but will greatly strengthen it.

197.

198.

197.

The sails are cut from the tissue using the plans for reference, but a little oversize as can be seen here. They can then be offered up to the relevant masts and spars and checked for fit before final trimming to size.

198.

Each sail is now shaped over a rounded surface, a technique expounded by the late Derek Hunniset, and I have used it for many years now. Here I am using part of an old plastic basin, but any smooth surface with the right curvature will suffice.

In practice water is applied to both sides of the sail and it is gently stretched to shape, smoothing out any wrinkles as you go. Splits are frequent, then you start again, hence the need to prepare extra sailcloth.

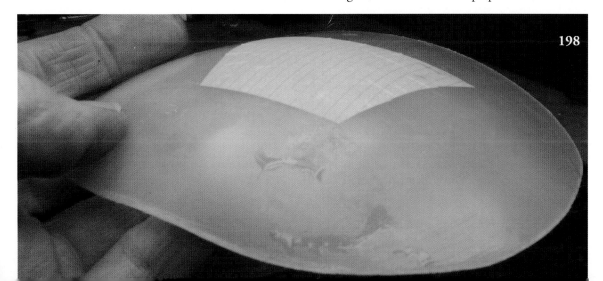

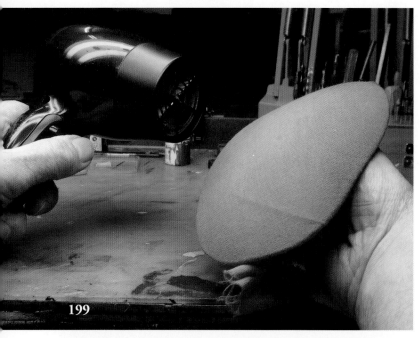

199.

When a satisfactory result has been achieved, the sail is covered with a cloth which is pulled tight, twisted and gripped with one hand while the other applies heat with a hair dryer. Experimentation will determine the length of time that it takes to dry the sail before starting to wrinkle it.

200.

The sail can then be lifted free and checked for blemishes. If it is all intact it can be returned to the mould for detailing. This involves fitting all the linings and reef bands. If the leech linings are left over long they can be glued to both sail and mould to keep the sail in place while detailing it (I use white glue) and then be trimmed free when the job is completed. The sail is then turned over and the tablings, bolt ropes and cringles added.

201

201.

The sail can then be glued to the yard. I have held them both in place here; it makes the whole job much easier. At this stage the spar should be detailed as described earlier and any reef points that are required fitted.

202.

The spanker not only needs to be glued to the gaff but has to be glued to each of the wooden hoops around the mast. As each one is glued to the sail the edge of the sail should be given a little curve in the direction of the wind before gluing to the next one. On my model the foot of the sail has been trimmed by hoisting the tack. I have come across this feature many times in copies of contemporary engravings, so it must have been quite commonplace. Whether it was to improve visibility, allow the wind to fill another sail or just a way of reducing sail I do not know, but it makes an attractive feature and also gives a clearer view of the deck with its fittings. The shaping is achieved by dampening the sail whilst concertinaing and teasing it to the desired shape. The curves are relatively easy to form, and should hold their shape well with the stiffening effect of the wire bolt ropes.

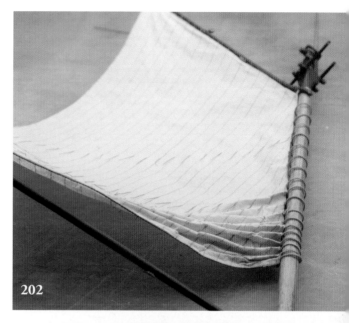

202

203.

The jibs are all fitted to their respective stays by means of rope hanks. These short lengths of wire are initially glued to one side of the sail, which is then turned over, the stay laid over them, and the hanks bent round the stay to the other side of the sail, where, if need be, they are trimmed before a touch of superglue fixes them in place. I have shown the flying jib in the process of being hoisted. Instead of being mounted to the stay by the hanks I have formed them round a rather more rigid length of wire which was then glued to the chipboard frame while shaping the sail. When I was satisfied with the result the wire was withdrawn from the hanks and the stay inserted.

Although shaping a sail in this way has its difficulties, it gives, in my opinion, more life to a model, a greater feeling of realism and atmosphere, and besides, it is very satisfying and great fun to do, which is, of course, what it is all about.

203

This just about concludes my task of describing the construction of these two models. Anything that I have failed to make clear should be readily made so by referring to the plans or one of the volumes in the bibliography.

The photographs of the completed models of *Neufchatel* should also help in this direction. I know

that in my early days as a modelmaker, good photographs of models were one of my greatest research assets, helping me to understand and interpret complicated and confusing plans.

The waterline model of *Neufchatel* is displayed in a glass case finished with Lacewood veneer, and the full-hull model in one finished with Myrtle Burr veneer.

⟨⟨Model Gallery ∾⟩⟩

Lynx & Musquedobet –1812

Length of hull: 6⅜ in

Overall length: As *Lynx*: 12¾ in, as *Musquedobet* 11in

The American schooner *Lynx* was built in 1812 as a privateer but was actually only employed as a blockade runner until her capture in 1813 by boats of sir John Warren's squadron. She was then taken into the Royal Navy, refitted, and renamed *Musquedobet*,

    I have built two models of her: one as *Lynx*, under sail, with her original armament of six 6pdr cannon, and the other as *Musquedobet*, fitted with a capstan and rearmed with eight 18pdr carronades and two 6pdr long guns. This second model shows her at anchor with a hoy alongside discharging water barrels. As the hatches of both schooner and hoy are uncovered, both hulls have been hollowed out from underneath and a false bottom fitted, allowing a glimpse of the details below.

Surly – 1806

Length of hull: 4⁷⁄₁₆ in

Overall length: 7⅜ in

If your interest veers towards the Royal Navy you could do worse than choose a cutter for a first model; they have so much character and interest with busy decks and a simple rig. The plans I used were the Admiralty draughts from the National Maritime Museum for the *Cheerful* class, backed up with information from Bill Shoulder's articles in *Model Shipwright* Nos 1 and 2. More information on rigging these little ships can be found in *Rigging Period Fore-and-Aft Craft* by Lennarth Petersson, *Eighteenth-Century Rigs and Rigging* by Karl Marquardt, and *The Art of Rigging* by George Biddlecombe.

Grasshopper – 1806

Length of hull: 6¾in

Overall length: 10¾in

A rather more advanced project would be a brig. The general construction would follow that for *Neufchatel* but the two fully-rigged square masts would make the project rather more ambitious. Of all the brig classes, one of the *Cruizer* class would seem to be an obvious choice. There is a contemporary model in the National Maritime Museum, and the excellent book *Modelling the Brig-of-War Irene* by E W Petrejus contains all the information and plans that you could need.

Washington – 1837

Length of hull: 6⅜ in

Overall length: 9½ in

Another similar subject would be the revenue cutter *Washington*. She was originally rigged as a schooner but was re-rigged as a brig in 1838. She has a rather more complicated deck layout with the after-house extending right across the ship, forming a raised deck, abaft of which was a sunken poop. She also has the extra interest of a pivoting 6pdr amidships, raised to fire over the bulwarks. A set of plans by William L Crothers is available from Rocky Mountain Shipyard.

America – *c*1851

Length of hull: 6⁵⁄₁₆ in

Overall length: 8½ in

This famous American schooner, which beat all-comers off Cowes in 1851 and became the first winner of what would become the America's Cup, would be another contender for a model built using the same methods as those described in this book. Details of her history, and plans, can be found in *The History of American Sailing Ships* by Howard Chapelle. A set of plans by William L Crothers is available from Rocky Mountain Shipyard.

❧ Epilogue ❧

Although less dramatic and imposing than a frigate or a ship-of-the-line, the smaller naval craft such as those featured in these pages are not only wonderful and fascinating subjects in their own right, but are ideal subjects for the beginner for the reasons mentioned in the Introduction. I would not, however, wish to give the impression that building miniature ship models is a discipline that should be embarked upon lightly, or in the expectation of easy and instant results, as many skills are involved.

Before even embarking on a model it is necessary to be able to read a set of plans, and for anyone new to ship modelling there is no better explanation of this topic than that to be found in *Modelling the Brig-of-War Irene* by E W Petrejus. Then, of course, there are the basic carving skills, the use of hand and power tools (and crucially, but frequently forgotten, the ability to sharpen and care for them). After all, a knife, chisel or plane is only as good as the man who sharpens it. Then there is the mixing and the application of paint and stain, something that can make or mar a model. As well as these basics you will need to work with wire, paper and tissue.

If you have made it this far through the book you will have witnessed the many processes involved in building these two models. Mastering the techniques involved is in large part what model building is all about, for, as well as the pleasure gleaned from contemplating the fruits of your labours, you will also have the added satisfaction of developing both practical, artistic and problem-solving skills that cannot fail to spill over into other areas of life. The rewards are great, and as with many things in this life, commensurate with the efforts and application that you bestow on them. No one expects to be able to drive a car instantly or find their way round a computer, but just as in model building, the more you learn, and particularly the more you practice, the better you become.

Do not be disheartened by photographs of my workshop and the array of tools and facilities that I have at my disposal. I am now a professional model builder and have spent many years acquiring them. Many of them are actually luxury items and in no way essential for the building of good models. Indeed, I have not always had a workshop, and, when first married, built my models on a wooden tray on a little coffee table in the living room. I sat on the floor with my legs straight out beneath it. When we moved house we aspired to a full-size table (home-made) and I was able to sit on a chair; I remember this as the height of luxury as it spared me many of the aches and pains my previous arrangement caused. Even as recently as 1989, by which time I had become a single parent, I was doing much of the work on my model of the frigate *Diana* on the living-room table, between keeping an eye on the boys and cooking dinner.

One thing that has changed dramatically over the past forty years is the plethora of books and plans now available, covering almost any area of ship modelling in which you might be interested. Back then there were the models and books by Harold Underhill, Norman Ough and, of course, Donald McNarry. These men were, even at a book's remove, my mentors, and I owe them a great debt.

I would like to think that in some small way I am adding to their legacy, and that somewhere out there this volume may help others towards a hobby or, who knows, even a career as rewarding as mine has been.

Good luck.

⊗ Materials and Tools ⊗

Below is a list of the suppliers of tools and materials, some of which have been mentioned in the text. I have not listed the suppliers of paints, adhesives, Milliput, Plasticine etc, as they are readily available in most arts and graphics shops or hardware stores and the types used are frequently dependent on personal choice.

In the UK

Airbrush & Spray Centre Ltd,
39 Littlehampton Road,
Worthing, West Sussex BN13 1QJ
Tel 08700 660445, E-mail airbrush@lineone.net
All your airbrush needs.

Ashley Iles (Edge Tools) Ltd,
East Kirkby,
Spilsby, Lincolnshire PE23 4DD
Tel (01790) 763372, Fax (01790) 763610
For chisels, gouges and some excellent sharpening materials.

Claudius Ash Sons & Co Ltd,
Summit House, Summit Road,
Potters Bar, Hertfordshire EN6 3EE
Tel (Free Phone) 0800 090909, Fax (01707) 649001
An excellent source of supply of the very fine diamond burs that figure prominently in the photographs.

Craft Supplies Ltd,
Newburgh Works, Netherside,
Bradwell, Derbyshire 533 9NT
Tel (01298) 871636, Fax ((01298) 872263,
E-mail sales@craft-supplies.co.uk
For many tools and timbers.

Douglas Electronic Industries Ltd,
55 Eastfield Road,
Louth, Lincs LN11 7AL
Tel (01507) 603643
Supplier of suitable transformer for use in the UK, along with the Preac Saw.

Falkiners,
76 Southampton Row,
London, WC1B 4AR
Tel 020 7831 1151
For supplies of Seccotine.

General Woodwork Supplies (Stoke Newington) Ltd,
76-80 Stoke Newington High Street,
London N16 7PA
Tel 020 7254 6052, Fax 020 7254 7223
Suppliers of most timbers, which they will cut to your own requirements. I have for many years used their Brazilian boxwood; it is very fine grained, takes stain well and can be brought to an excellent finish. They can usually supply lemonwood.

H S Walsh,
21 Cross St, Hatton Garden,
London EC1N 8UN
Tel (020 7242 3711
Suppliers of tools for the jewellery trade including tweezers and very fine files.

John Boddy Timber Ltd,
Riverside Sawmills,
Boroughbridge, North Yorkshire YO51 9LJ
Tel (01423) 322370, Fax (01423) 323810
A good general timber supplier, including jelutong.

Maynard Ltd,
Merretts Mill,
Woodchester, Gloucestershire GL5 5EX
Tel (01453) 833185.
Suppliers and repairers of Emco and Unimat lathes.

Ormiston Wire Ltd,
1 Fleming Way,
Worton Road,
Isleworth, Middlesex TW7 6EU
Tel (020) 8569 728, Fax (020) 8569 8601,
E-mail info@ormiston-wire.ac.uk
Suppliers of most types of wire including the tinned copper that I have made extensive use of on this model.

Pintail Bird Carvings,
David and Sheila Clews,
20 Sheppenhall Grove,
Aston, Nantwich, Cheshire CW5 8DF
Tel (01270) 780056, Fax (01270) 780056
For carbide, diamond and ruby cutters. They can also supply jelutong, which they are usually prepared to cut to your own specifications.

Squires Model and Craft Tools,
100, London Road,
Bognor Regis, West Sussex, PO21 1DD
Tel 01243 842424, Fax 01243842525
Suppliers of Minicraft tools, and many of the other model supplies that you are likely to need.

Swann-Morton Ltd,
Owleton Green, Sheffield S6 2BJ
Tel 0114 2344231, Fax (0114) 231 4966
Suppliers of scalpels, knives and blades. I particularly like their SM-00 knife used with the SM01 blade.

Timberline,
Unit 7, Munday Works,
58- 66 Morley Road,
Tonbridge, Kent TN9 IRP
Tel (01732) 355626, Fax (01732) 358214
Timbers including lemonwood.

In the US

Lumber Yard,
6908 Stadium Drive,
Brecksville OH 44141
E-mail: Bodyplan@aol.com
Has a wide range of woods.

Micro-Mark,
340-2656 Snyder Avenue,
Berkeley Heights, NJ 07922
Tel 1 800 225 1066
Good supplier of a great variety of tools.

Preac Tool Co, Inc,
1596 Pea Pond Road, North Bellmore,
New York, NY 11710
Tel 516 333 1500, Fax 5116 333 1501,
E-mail: preac@crols.com
For the excellent miniature precision table saw, thicknesses etc.

Warner Woods West,
P O Box 100,
Irvins, UT 84738
Tel 435 652 4400
For wood supplies.

The following are good suppliers of general modelling materials.
Ace Surgical Supply Co Inc,
1034 Pearl Street,
Brockton MA 02301
Tel 800 583 3100

K&S Engineering,
6917 W 59th Street,
Chicago, IL 60638
Tel 773 586 8503

Pelican Wire Co Inc,
White Lake Corporate Park,
3650 Shaw Blvd,
Naples, Florida 34117
Tel 239 597 8555

Small Parts Inc,
13980 NW 58th Court,
Miami Lakes FL 33014-0650
Tel 305 558 1038

⧉ *Further Reading* ⧉

Below is a list of books, periodicals and catalogues which I have found to be useful sources of information during the construction of this and many other models.
 Some knowledge of ships and their rigs is, if not essential, then highly desirable, and will only add to the satisfaction gained when undertaking the building of a model.

Chapelle, Howard Irving, *The History of American Sailing Ships* (New York 1982)
——————, *The History of the American Sailing Navy* (New York 1949)

Harland, John and Myers, Mark, *Seamanship in the Age of Sail* (London 1984)

Lavery. Brian, *The Arming and Fitting of English Ships of War 1600-1815* (London 1987)

Lees, James. *The Masting and Rigging of English Ships of War 1625 – 1860* (London 1979)

Marquardt, Karl Heinz. *Eighteenth-Century Rigs and Rigging* (London 1992)
——————, *The Global Schooner* (London 2003)

May W E, *The Boats of Men-of-War* (London 1999)

Petersson, Lennarth, *Rigging Period Ship Models* (London 2000)
——————-, *Rigging Period Fore-and-Aft Craft* (London 2007)

Petrejus, E W *Modelling the Brig-of-War Irene* (Hengalo, Holland 1970)

The plans for *Neufchatel* were supplied by: The Smithsonian Institution,
Washington D C 20560
Ships Plans, Naval
NMH-5010/MRC628